Basics of Layer-2 LAN Switching

A Switching Guide for BSIT Students of Network Systems Track

Mudzramer A. Hayudini, MPA, CCAI

Basics of Layer-2 LAN Switching

A Switching Guide for BSIT Students of Network Systems Track

All rights reserved

Copyright @2021 by

Mudzramer A. Hayudini

This book may contain codes, configurations, and excerpts the use of which may not have been pre-authorized. The material is made for educational purposes. The contents do not intend to replace any official books or materials used for CCNA or the academy, and that the ideas found inside the book belong to its respective owners.

This book is not sponsored by or endorsed by or affiliated with Cisco Systems, Inc., Cisco®, Cisco Systems®, Cisco Networking Academy™, CCNA™, the Cisco Systems logo are trademarks or registered trademarks of Cisco Systems, Inc. in the United States and other countries. All other copyrights and trademarks mentioned herein are the possession of their respective owners. The author and the publisher do not claim ownership by the mention of products that contain these marks.

The author and the publisher make no representations of any kind in connection to the contents' accuracy and accept no liability of any kind, including but not limited to losses or damages of any kind caused directly or indirectly from this book.

Published by

Lulu Press Inc.

United States of America

ISBN 978-1-7947-1339-0

DEDICATION

This book is dedicated to all BSIT students of Mindanao State University-Sulu, the key asset of the Information Technology Department. They motivated me to pursue my mission to introduce technology that the province has never experienced. Their reward is a better future for themselves, their family, and their province. I have hope in you.

ACKNOWLEDGMENTS

The first person whom I would like to thank and acknowledge is my Mentor, Engr. Roy L. Pamitalan for guiding and teaching me everything about Network Systems. Sir, you are such an incredible Trainer; you helped me to reach where I am today.

I acknowledge the Mindanao State University-Sulu family, particularly the College of Computer Studies, for the great job in motivating me. I got the book idea from my colleagues.

The Cisco Networking Academy Program is a guide and basis for creating this book and the primary source of my technical knowledge in Network Systems.

Thank you, Mr. Nickmar Asjali, for the assistance you extended to me during the creation of this book.

To my family, friends, and the love of my life for supporting me financially and emotionally, thank you.

To my family, friends, and the love of my life, thank you for supporting me financially and emotionally.

And lastly, heartfelt gratitude to the Almighty God, Allah S.W.T., whom all of these are nothing without Him.

Contents at a Glance

	Introduction	viii
Dedication		ii
Acknowledgements		iii
Table of Contents		iv
Chapter 1	Layer 2 Switching	1
Chapter 2	LAN Switch Types	13
Chapter 3	Basic Switch Management	19
Chapter 4	Layer 2 Switching	49
Chapter 5	Virtual Local Area Network	88
Chapter 6	VLAN Trunking Protocol	99
Chapter 7	Inter-VLAN Communication	103
Chapter 8	EtherChannel	111
Chapter 9	Basic Telephony Service	123
	Glossary	130
	References	135

Table of Contents

CHAPTER 1   **Layer 2 Switching**   1
- LAN Switching Concepts   2
- Ethernet Networking   3
- Ethernet at the Data Link Layer   3
- MAC Addressing   3
- Ethernet Frames   4
- Limitations of Layer-2 Switching   5
- Difference between Bridging and LAN Switching   5
- Switch Functions at Layer 2   5

CHAPTER 2   **LAN Switch Types**   15
- Types of Switch   15
- Symmetric and Asymmetric Switching   17
- Switching Methods   19

CHAPTER 3   **Basic Switch Management**   21
- Switch Boot Sequence   21
- Switch Recovery from System Crash   22
- Switch LED Indicators   22
- Switch Basic Configuration   23
- Verifying Configurations   33
- Switch Security   36

CHAPTER 4   **Layer 2 Switching**   47
- Spanning-Tree Protocol   47
- Bridge Protocol Data Unit   54
- PortFast   60
- UplinkFast   65
- BackboneFast   68

Rapid Spanning-Tree Protocol	70
Multiple Spanning-Tree Protocol	75

CHAPTER 5 Virtual Local Area Network — 85

- Flat Network — 85
- Virtual Local Area Network (802.1Q) — 86
- Benefits of VLAN — 88
- VLAN Memberships — 89
- Switching Link Types — 91
- How VLAN Works — 92
- Introduction to Dynamic Trunking Protocol — 93

CHAPTER 6 VLAN Trunking Protocol — 95

- VTP Modes — 95
- Configuration Revision Number — 96
- VTP Pruning — 97

CHAPTER 7 Inter-VLAN Communication — 99

- Inter-VLAN Routing Operation — 99
- Router-on-a-Stick Inter-VLAN Routing — 100
- Inter-VLAN Routing in Layer 3 Switch — 103

CHAPTER 8 EtherChannel — 107

- EtherChannel Operation — 107
- Port Aggregation Protocol — 109
- Link Aggregation Control Protocol — 112

CHAPTER 9 Basic Telephony Service — 119

- Introduction to Voice over IP — 119
- Voice VLAN — 119
- Call Manager Express — 122

Glossary — 125

References — 130

vii

Introduction

Basics of Layer-2 LAN Switching: A Switching Guide for BSIT Students of Network Systems Track is designed to aid the students in understanding the concepts of switching in the Cisco environment easily.

This book introduces and extends the students' knowledge and practical experience, enabling them to develop the important skills related to designing and configuring LAN and maintaining switches. The concepts discussed in this book empower the students to be prepared, execute standards, and design networks in the ideal approach through implementing best switching practices.

The Goal of this Book

This book aims to educate students about Cisco technologies and help them understand how a network is being created and designed and how Cisco devices are being configured. It is used as an aggregated reference for BSIT major in networks systems.

The audience for this book

This book is written for BSIT majors in Network Systems of Higher Education Institutions and a guide for IT Instructors. This book could be used as a guide or textbook in the classroom and in laboratory sessions as a lab manual.

Organization of the book

This book is organized according to the following divisions:

Chapter 1 presents an overview of the layer-2 switching concepts and some switching terminologies.

Chapter 2 presents an overview of the different switching modes.

Chapter 3 covers the basic switching configuration to manage a Cisco switch

Chapter 4 discusses the PortFast, BPDU guard, BPDU filter, UplinkFast, BackboneFast, and loop guard spanning-tree enhancement on the catalyst enterprise LAN switches. This also covers the STP, RSTP, and MSTP.

Chapter 5 provides information regarding the process of Virtualizing Local Area Networking, its advantages, and its benefits.

Chapter 6 discuss the VTP process as a technique for VLAN creation

Chapter 7 covers the Inter-VLAN communication of each VLAN using a router.

Chapter 8 discuss the concepts of Link aggregation or EtherChannel, the standards of Link bonding accepted in the field.

Chapter 9 covers the configuration and basics of VOIP telephony service in the VLAN setup

Layer 2 Switching

CHAPTER 1

LAN Switching Concepts

Switching usually takes place at layer 2 of the OSI Model. Since it is at layer 2, switching is hardware-based which means it uses the MAC address from the PC or host's network interface card to filter the network. Application-Specific Integrated Circuits (ASICs), an integrated circuit (IC) chip, is what the switches use to create and maintain the table for switching decisions. Since layer-2 switches are MAC-based, it only considers the Frame's MAC Addresses. Because of that, they are fast for the need to look at the network layer header information (Packet Header) is no longer required. Layer-2 switching provides hardware-based bridging (MAC), wire-speed, low latency, and low cost.

> **Terminologies:**
>
> **Latency** – also called propagation delay, is the period or the time a frame or packet takes to transmit from the source host to its destination on the network.
>
> **Cost** – refers to the link path cost. Each link used with different types of cable has its own unique path cost basing from the IEEE standards

Layer-2 switching is efficient for it only modifies the frame encapsulating the packet and not the data packet itself. Since no modification occurs on the part of the data packet, the switching process is faster and promotes less error than routing.

Layer-2 switching is typically used for workgroup connectivity similar to a Computer Laboratory setup. It is also used in network segmentation. This type of setup allows you to establish a flat network rather than those 10BaseT traditional shared networks. Another unique characteristic about Layer-2 switching is that it increases each user or host connected to the device. The reason behind this is that every port or interface in the switch has its collision domain, so you can connect multiple devices to each interface without being exposed to data collisions.

> **Note:**
>
> 10BaseT is a 10 mbps baseband Ethernet specification using two pairs of twisted-pair cabling (Category 3, 4, 5): one pair for transmitting data and other for receiving data. 10BaseT, which is part of the IEEE 802.3 specification, has a distance limit of approximately 100 meters per segment (Source: Cisco Networking Academy Program: Second-Year Companion guide, Cisco Press.)

> **Terminologies:**
>
> **Network Segmentation** – process of breaking down collision domain
> **Packet** – is the layer 3 letter which contains logical addresses
> **Frame** – is the layer 2 envelope/letter which contains physical addresses
> **Collision Domain** – the area in which frames are propagated and have collided.

Ethernet Networking

According to Cisco Networking Academy official press, Ethernet is a baseband LAN specification invented by Xerox Corporation and developed jointly by Xerox, Intel, and Digital Equipment Corporation. Ethernet networks use CSMA/CD and run over a variety of cable types at 10 Mbps. It is similar to the IEEEE 802.3 series of standards. Ethernet is a media access method that allows all hosts to share the same bandwidth of a link. The Ethernet became popular because it is easy to troubleshoot and implement. Some technologies were evolved from Ethernet, such as FastEthernet and GigabitEthernet.

Ethernet at the Data Link Layer

The book "Cisco Certified Network Associate Study Guide" by Mr. Todd Lame discussed that Ethernet is responsible in various ways at the Data Link Layer. To mention some, Ethernet at layer 2 is responsible for MAC Addressing. It Is also tasked with framing packets received from the Network Layer and preparing them for transmission on the local network through the Ethernet Contention media access method. Ethernet frames have different types of frames available such as:

- Ethernet_II
- IEEE 802.3
- IEEE 802.2
- SNAP

MAC Addressing

The Media Access Control (MAC) Address, sometimes called physical or hardware address, is a 48-bit address written in a standard Hexadecimal format to ensure that addresses are of the same form even if different LAN technologies are used. Below is the content of the 48-bit address.

The IEEE assigns the Organizationally Unique Identifier (OUI) to an organization (24bits or 3bytes). The organization, in turn, assigns a globally administered address (24bits or 3bytes) that is unique (supposedly) to every adapter they manufacture. Notice bit 46. Bit 46 must be 0 if it is a globally assigned bit from the manufacturer and 1 if it is locally administered from the network administrator. *(Cisco Certified Network Associate Study Guide, Todd Lamle).*

Figure 1-1 MAC Address

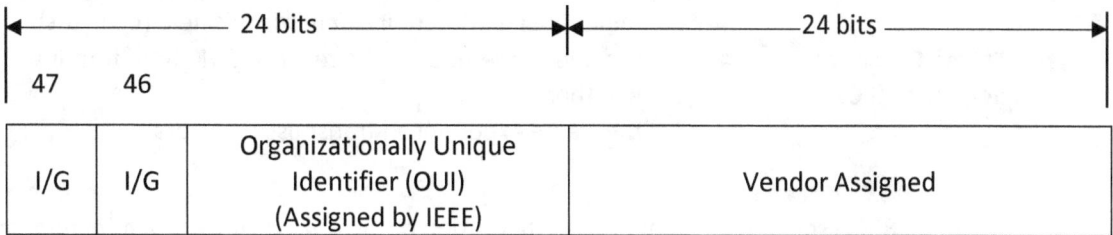

Ethernet Frames

Layer 2 of the OSI model, the Data Link Layer, combines bits into bytes and bytes into frames. Each layer of the OSI has its unique logical groupings; for Layer 2, the Frame serves as its logical grouping of information sent to the data link layer unit over a transmission medium. They are used to encapsulate packets handed down from the Network layer.

The Ethernet data-link protocol defines ethernet frame in the following order of format:

- Front: Ethernet Header
- Middle: Encapsulated data
- Back: Ethernet Trailer

However, the complete form of the frame *(Commonly Used Ethernet Frame form)* is defined below:

Figure 1-2 Ethernet Frame

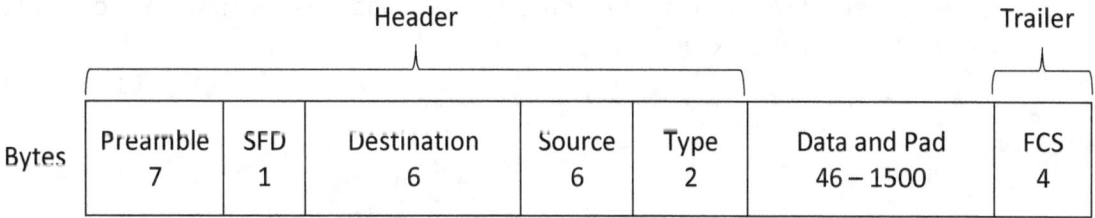

Table 1-1 IEEE 802.3 Ethernet Header and Trailer Fields

Field	Bytes	Description
Preamble	7	Synchronization.
Start Frame Delimiter (SFD)	1	Signifies that the next byte begins the Destination MAC Address field.
Destination MAC Address	6	Identifies the intended recipient of this frame.

Source MAC Address	6	Identifies the sender of this frame.
Type	2	Defines the type of protocol listed inside the frame; today, most likely identifies IP version 4 (IPv4) or IP version 6 (IPv6).
Data and Pad*	46–1500	Holds data from a higher layer, typically an L3PDU (usually an IPv4 or IPv6 packet). The sender adds padding to meet the minimum length requirement for this field (46 bytes).
Frame Check Sequence (FCS)	4	Provides a method for the receiving NIC to determine whether the frame experienced transmission errors.

* The IEEE 802.3 specification limits the data portion of the 802.3 frames to a minimum of 46 and a maximum of 1500 bytes. The *term maximum transmission unit* (MTU) defines the maximum Layer 3 packet sent over a medium. Because the Layer 3 packet rests inside the data portion of an Ethernet frame, 1500 bytes is the largest IP MTU allowed over an Ethernet *(Source: CCNA 201-301: Official Cert Guide Vol.1, Wendell Odom).*

Limitations of Layer-2 Switching

Since switches are somehow similar to bridges, keep in mind that switches may also possess the same problems as those of bridged networks. When designed properly, Bridges are good in breaking up the collision domain; thus, you can say that 80 percent reliability of the user's time is spent on the local segment *(Cisco Certified Network Associate Study Guide, Todd Lamle).*

It may have broken the collision domain, but the network is still one broadcast domain. Layer-2 switches can't break up the broadcast domain, which therefore can cause performance issues such as imposing limitations on the size of your network. Bear in mind that broadcast and multicast and the slow convergence of spanning trees can lead to serious problems as the network expands. With these presented issues, layer-2 switches cannot completely remove and replace routers (layer-3 devices) in the internetwork; hence, both devices must work together to attain a well-performing network fully.

Figure 1-3 A network with 4 collision domains and 1 broadcast domain

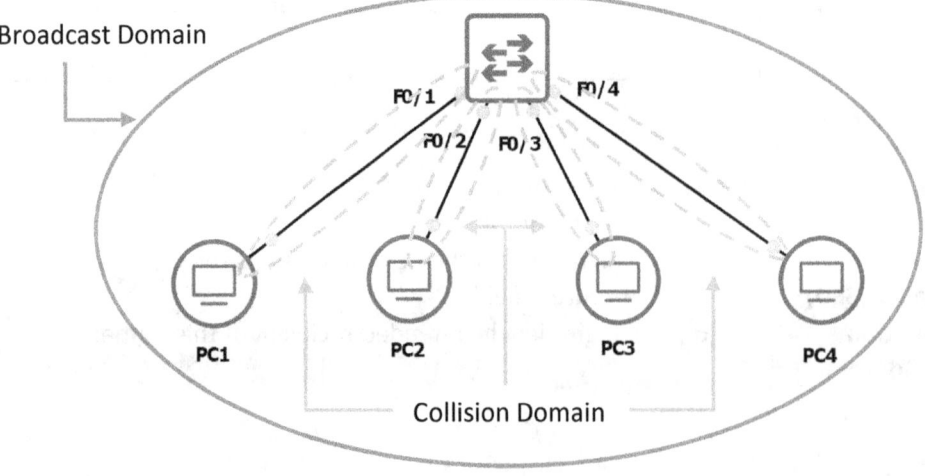

Difference between Bridging and LAN Switching

You might be wondering the difference between bridging and switching; well, the following are some of the key points that determine the differences between the two: *(Cisco Certified Network Associate Study Guide, Todd Lamle).*

- Bridges are software-based, which requires a configuration to interconnect the devices connected on its interface fully. At the same time, switches are hardware-based because it uses an ASICs chip to help make filtering decisions.
- Bridges can only have one spanning-tree instance per bridge, while switches can have many.
- In the MikroTik approach, Bridges has complete visibility of all port's statistics compared to switching that has no visibility of traffic on slave ports

Switch Functions at Layer 2

How do switches do the switching process? Switches do their job by completing several functions. These functions are what have made them be called a LAN switch. The role of a LAN switch is to forward Ethernet frames. Of course, LANs exist when there are different types of devices, whether a PC, server, or any other devices that connect to switches, with the switches connected.

The primary job of the switch is to forward frames based on its destination address. And to accomplish that job, switches formulated a sequence of patterns which then explains how the switch looks upon the frame's Ethernet header. This sequence of the pattern is the logic embedded in every switch on the market. LAN switches are receiving ethernet frames, and then it's up to the LAN switches to make a decision. The decision under the switching methods is forwarding, which delivers the frame to some of the ports or just drops the frame by ignoring it.

To easily understand how the decision-making is being done, there are three (3) distinct functions of layer-2 switching:

1. **Forward/ Filter Decision** – this is where the exact decision takes place. When a frame is received on an interface, the switch examines the destination hardware address and finds the exit interface in the CAM table.
2. **Address Learning** – Switches and bridges record the source hardware address of each frame received on an interface by examining them and entering the data into the *Content Address Memory (CAM) table*. If addresses are already entered on the table, forwarding of frames can now be prepared.
3. **Loop avoidance** – One copy of the frame is being prepared to forward to the destination by establishing a loop avoidance scheme with other switches using Spanning-tree Protocol.

Out of the three functions, the primary job of the switch is the first function. The two are just overhead functions of the switch.

Forwarding/ Filter Decisions

Every frame received by the switch on any interface, its destination MAC address is compared to the CAM table. The rule is, if the address is present on the table, the frame is only sent out on the interface where the destination is located and does not transmit the frame to any other exit interface. Because of this, bandwidth is preserved on the other network segment. This process is called *Frame Filtering.*

However, if the destination MAC address is nowhere to be found on the table, then broadcast of the frame takes place on all active interfaces except the interface where the frame originated. If a device answers the broadcast, the CAM table is updated with the destination's location, the interface where it is placed. Usually, broadcast on the switch occurs when the switch has its first power up or is rebooting.

Figure 1-4 Switch forwarding and Filtering

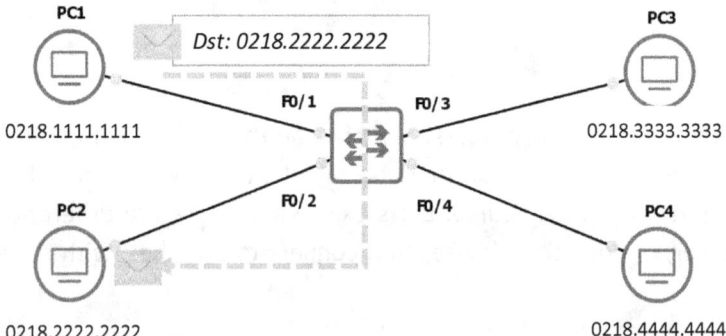

MAC Address	Interface
0218.1111.1111	F0/1
0218.2222.2222	F0/2
0218.3333.3333	F0/3
0218.4444.4444	F0/4

Let us consider figures 1-4; PC 1 sends a frame to PC2 with a destination MAC address of 0218.2222.2222. (1) Basically, the switch receives the frame in port F0/1, as the frame travels on the switch, (2) the CAM table is now being examined if the MAC address is present, if the address is listed on the table, it will now check as to where the correct exit interface should be sent so that the frame will be delivered properly. (3) In this case, the MAC address is listed on the table; thus, the switch will now forward the frame to the port where PC2 is located, which is F0/2. After successfully transmitting the frame, (4) the switch will proceed to the filter decision where the switch will no longer send and consider any other interface as its recipient.

What happens if there two or more switches on a network? Let us consider figure 1-4

Figure 1-5 Forwarding and Filtering with two Switches involved

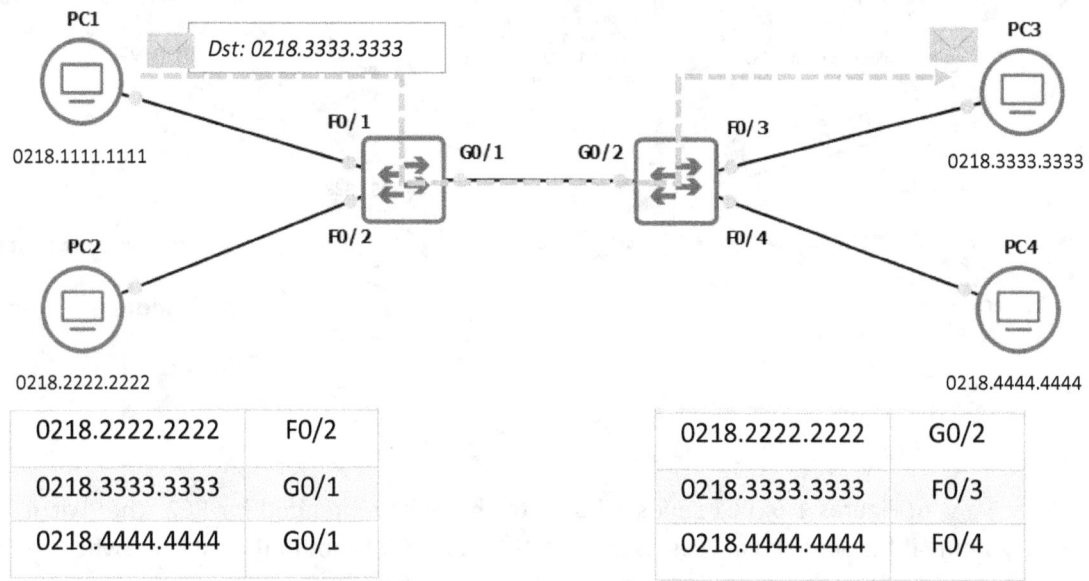

0218.2222.2222	F0/2
0218.3333.3333	G0/1
0218.4444.4444	G0/1

0218.2222.2222	G0/2
0218.3333.3333	F0/3
0218.4444.4444	F0/4

If there are two or more switches involved, the switching process is still the same. The switch will still need to check the frame from the source. We will change the previous example we had; PC1 is trying to send a frame to PC3 this time. For the switching process, the logic is still the same. The frame arrives at F0/1 on switch 1, then it sees the destination at G0/2, and it will be forwarded to that interface. After that, switch 2 CAM table will be used; at Switch 2, the same frame arrives at G0/2 and will be forwarded to F0/3.

Address Learning

By default, when a switch is powered on, its CAM table is empty. The switch learns the addresses of all connected devices when the devices start to send frames. It builds the CAM table by listening to incoming frames and examining the source MAC Address in the frame. If the address is not listed on the table, the switch creates an entry and records the MAC address and the location or interface of the source device. When the CAM table is complete, the switch can make an accurate switching decision.

Let us consider the previous figure we had.

Figure 1-6 (1) PC1 will send a frame

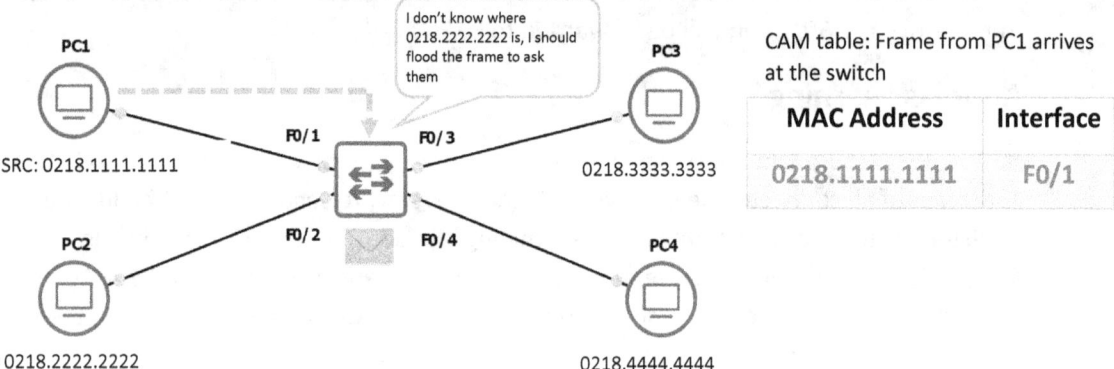

CAM table before frame is sent

MAC Address	Interface
<empty>	<empty>

CAM table: frame arrives at the switch

MAC Address	Interface
0218.1111.1111	F0/1

In Figures 1-6, PC1 sends a frame to the switch intended for PC2. The switch will now examine if the sender's address is in the CAM table; if it is not in the list, the switch will add the source MAC address of the frame and the Interface where it was received.

After adding the source, the switch will now check the destination address in the table.

Figure 1-6 (2) The switch will check the destination address in the table

CAM table: Frame from PC1 arrives at the switch

MAC Address	Interface
0218.1111.1111	F0/1

If It is not in the table, the switch will flood the frame to all connected interfaces, asking the owner.

Figure 1-7 explains the process.

Figure 1-7 (3) Switch will flood the frame

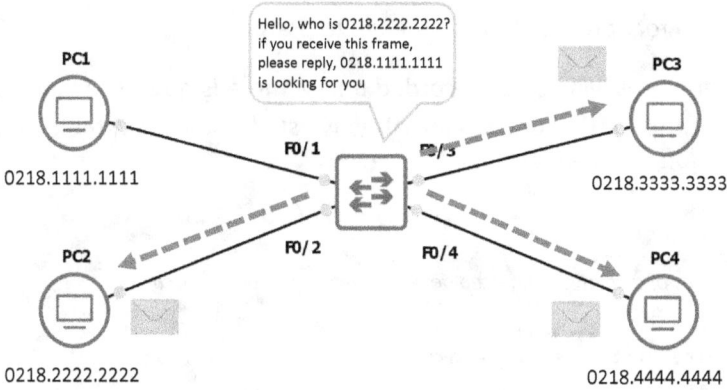

Of course, since the PCs already received the frame, frames not intended for other PCs are discarded; only the real recipient will reply. Figure 1-8 shows the process.

Figure 1-8 (4) Frame is received by PC2, and is now ready to forward the frame

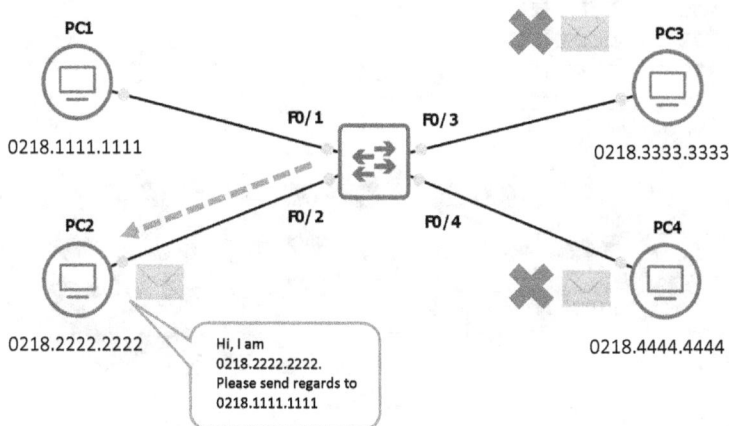

The switch will finally record the address of PC2 and will forward the reply frame back to PC1

Figure 1-9 (5) PC1 receives the reply from PC2

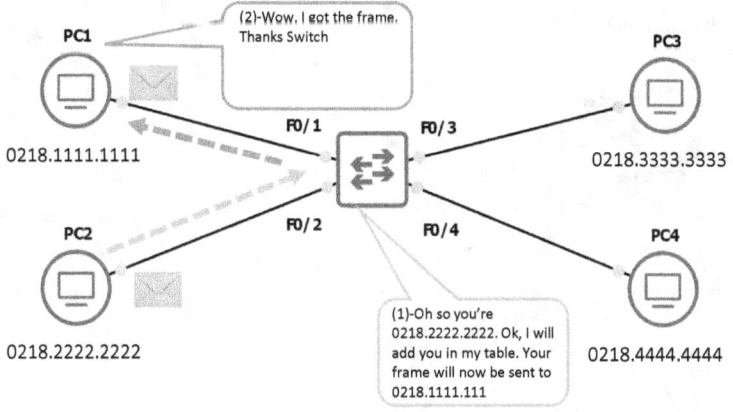

CAM table: Frame from PC2 arrives at the switch

MAC Address	Interface
0218.1111.1111	F0/1
0218.2222.2222	F0/2

The concept of switching is similar to the scenario of when a student loses his/her ID; the Guard will make an announcement, only the owner of the ID will reply to the guard, with his/her reply, he or she will be finally listed on the record book. When the CAM table is complete, PC2 will successfully reply to PC1, a forwarding of the frame is successful.

Remember, MAC addresses will not be recorded unless there is no transaction going on in the network. To monitor if the MAC addresses are already listed in the CAM table on a Cisco switch, the following commands are used:

Figure 1-10 Shows the MAC addresses of all active connected devices when a transaction occurs.

```
Switch3#show mac address-table dynamic
          Mac Address Table
-------------------------------------------

Vlan      Mac Address         Type        Ports
----      -----------         --------    -----

   1      0218.1111.1111      DYNAMIC     Fa0/1
   1      0218.2222.2222      DYNAMIC     Fa0/2
   1      0218.3333.3333      DYNAMIC     Fa0/3
   1      0218.4444.4444      DYNAMIC     Fa0/4
Switch3#!
```

> **Terminology:**
>
> *Flooding – it is similar to broadcast but take note that flooding is different from broadcast. Broadcast frames is sent to a Broadcast MAC address which is FFFF.FFFF.FFFF. while flooding happens when the destination is not listed on the table, thus switches or bridges will transmit a copy of the frame to every interface except on the interface where the traffic originated.*

In a real network infrastructure, it is good to have multiple links towards another device; the benefit of this is that in case 1 link fails, there is a backup path. This process is known as failover.

Figure 1-11 Two Switches with redundant link

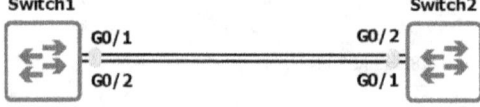

Figure 1-12 Four Switches with redundant link

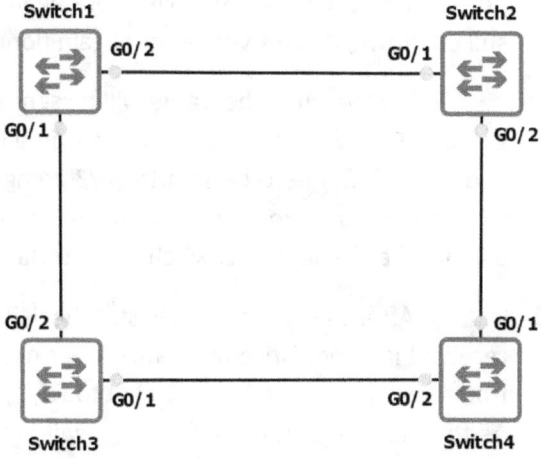

> **Note:**
>
> *Since we are using GNS3 for our network diagram, the links for switch to switch is represented with solid lines. For packet tracer, it is represented by dash or dotted line. In Cisco environment, when you are connecting switch to switch, we use crossover or cross-connect type of cable.*

But, when redundant network links are not properly managed, a loop can occur on the network because frames can be broadcasted down all redundant links simultaneously. Let us consider Figure 1-13 as our example.

Figure 1-13 Broadcast Storm

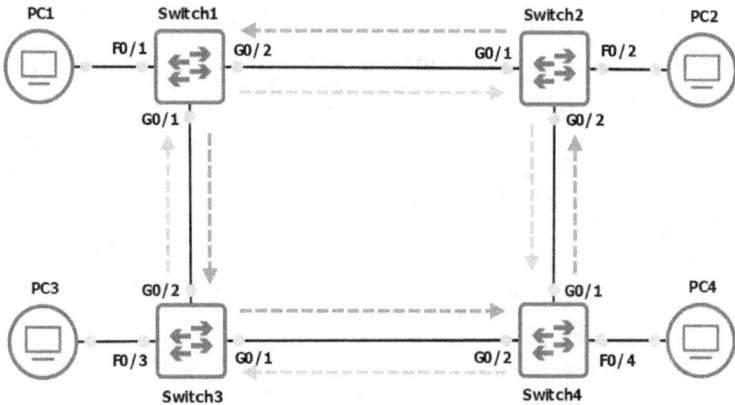

Let us say that PC1 is sending a frame to PC2; we assume that PC2 is off for this scenario. Since PC2 is off, its MAC address is not listed on the CAM table. Now, what will happen is that once the frame is received by switch 1 in interface F0/1, the switch will now look up for the destination's MAC address on the table. Since the address is nowhere to be found, it will flood the frame to all active interfaces. Since there are two links from switch one connected to other switches (G0/1, and G0/2), the frame will be sent over those links. The next thing is, switch 3

11

will receive the frame in interface G0/2, and Switch two will receive the frame in interface G0/1. Both Switch 2 and Switch 3 will check again its table for possible match-up, since the address is still unknown, these switches will again flood the frame.

For Switch 2, the frame will be sent to G0/2, which is going to Switch 4, and F0/2 which is going to PC2, while for Switch 3, the frame will be sent to G0/1, which is a link going to Switch 4 and another frame to be sent to F0/3 going to PC3. As the frame will now reach Switch 4, there will be two frames received. One from Switch 2 which was received by Switch 4 in interface G0/1, and another frame from Switch 3 in interface G0/2.

After that, switch 4 will still check its CAM table if the destination address of the frames received is listed. Since the frame is yet nowhere to be found, it will again flood the frame. The frame received in G0/2 will be sent to G0/1, and the frame received in G0/1 will be sent to G0/2. As the process continues, Switch 1 will receive again another two frames, and the process of checking the table will again continue that the frame to be sent will be doubled, thus creating a loop known as *Broadcast Storm*.

Aside from multiple frames being received by the devices resulting to loop, another problem that arises for this setup is that the CAM table will be confused as to where the device is since the switch can receive the frame from more than one link. Because of this, it is possible that the switch can't forward a frame because the table keeps on updating the source MAC address locations. This process is called *thrashing* the CAM table.

> Terminology:
>
> *Broadcast Storm – an undesirable event in which many broadcasts are sent simultaneously across all network segments. A broadcast storm uses substantial network bandwidth and, typically, causes network timeouts (Source: Cisco Networking Academy Program: Second-Year Companion guide, Cisco Press.)*

A manual solution to prevent the loop is to shut down at least one of the interfaces from the topology.

Figure 1-14 Manual solution: Shutdown one interface to prevent loop

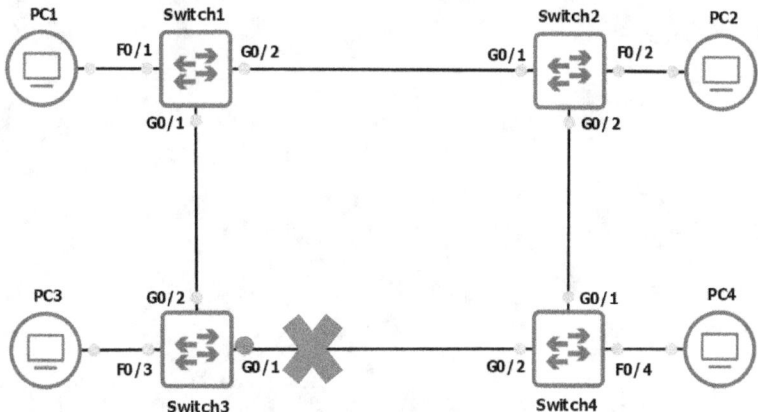

Figure 1-14 shows what will happen if you manually shutdown one of the interfaces from the topology. This is done through shutdown command in the cisco switch. Figure 1-115shows the configuration for this setup.

Figure 1-15 shutdown command at Switch3 in interface G0/1

```
Switch3>en
Switch3#config t
Enter configuration commands, one per line.  End with CNTL/Z.
Switch3(config)#int g0/1
Switch3(config-if)#shutdown

%LINK-5-CHANGED: Interface GigabitEthernet0/1, changed state to
administratively down
Switch3(config-if)#!
```

Though the commands are effective, remember, it is a good practice as a network administrator to let the switch do the job automatically, which means the switch will automatically detect and stop the network loop. That is why Spanning-Tree Protocol (STP) was invented. STP will be discussed in Chapter 4.

LAN Switch Types

CHAPTER 2

Types of Switch

The network is growing exponentially; as it grows, the network requirement is also changing. One should keep up with the changes to keep him/her updated. Knowing the different types of switches will help the network administrator find the right solution that can cope with future needs. Various categories of switches are available with unique benefits to consider as users explore their options.

Modular Switches

Modular Switches are switches that let the Network Administrator add expansion modules into the switches as needed, giving them flexibility as their need changes. Examples of modules that can be added are application-specific such as firewall, wireless, network analysis, and additional interfaces modules like cooling fans, SFP modules, and or power supplies.

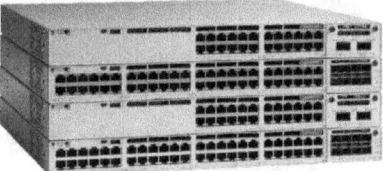

Figure 2-1 Cisco Catalyst 9300 Series Switch

Fixed Configuration Ethernet Switches

These are switches with a fixed number of ports and are not expandable. It can be further identified as Unmanaged switches, Smart Switches and Managed L2 and L3 Switches.

- **Unmanaged Switches**

    This type of switch is commonly known as plug-and-play switches since it is designed for basic connectivity. Switches under this category are widely used in Small-Office and Home-office (SOHO) networks.

Figure 2-2 Cisco Small Business 110 Series Unmanaged Switches

- **Smart Switches**

    This type of switch is evolving. They are lighter in capabilities and are less scalable than managed switches but can do some management such as QoS, VLAN, and Security. They can be deployed as edge switches of a large network, being the infrastructure for smaller networks or less complex environment needs.

Figure 2-3 Cisco 250 Series Smart Switches

- **Fully Managed L2 and L3 Switches**

    Managed switches are designed to provide the most comprehensive set of features to deliver the best services. It is more scalable, flexible, and precise in control and management of the network. They are usually deployed as access switches in the very large network or as core switches in relatively smaller networks. They are more secured than other switches since they are rich in features that enable them to be protected against DoS. Layer 3 switches also have routing capabilities and can support VRRP (Virtual Router Redundancy Protocol).

Figure 2-4 Cisco Catalyst 2960s-24TS Layer 2 Switch   *Figure 2-5 Cisco Catalyst 3560 Multilayer Series Switch*

Other Considerations

There are other options that can be considered when choosing the best switch for your network, this includes: Network switch speeds, number of ports, Power over Ethernet feature and stacking capabilities.

- **Network Switch Speeds** – available speed for fixed-configuration switches are Fast Ethernet (10/100 Mbps), Gigabit Ethernet (10/100/1000 Mbps), Ten Gigabit (10/100/1000/10000 Mbps), and even 40/100 Gbps speeds.
- **Number of Ports** – Available switch sizes are 5, 8, 10, 16, 24, 28, 48, and 52 ports; some comes with SFP/SFP+ slots for fiber connectivity
- **Power over Ethernet** – This capability can power up other devices such as IP CCTV Camera, Wireless Access Point, and VoIP Phones over a single cable. Switches can deliver power loading basing on the IEEEE standards of:
    - **IEEE 802.3af** – Delivers power up to 15.4 Watts
    - **IEEE 802.at** – Delivers power up to 30 Watts
    - **UPoE** – Delivers power up to 60 Watts
    - **IEEE 802.3bt** – Delivers power up to 100 Watts
- **Stackable VS Standalone Switches** – You might also consider a stackable switch compared to standalone switches, especially when handling multiple switches. Stackable switches are also fully functioning as standalone but can be set up to work and operate together with one or more other switches but manage them just like a single device.

Symmetric and Asymmetric Switching

Symmetric switching is a characteristic of a LAN switch that handles the same bandwidth allocation to each switch port.

Figure 2-6 Symmetric Switching with a total throughput of 40 Mbps

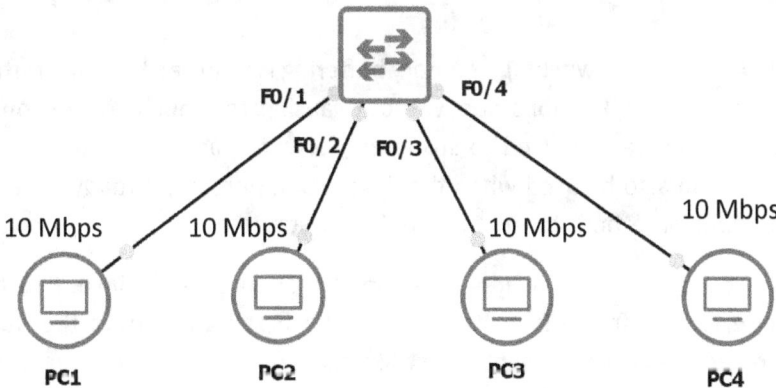

In the above figure, let us assume that the PCs are segmented. Each segment has a bandwidth of 10 Mbps; there is an even distribution of bandwidth across the entire network in the Symmetric switching. So, in this case, the total throughput is 40 Mbps.

Asymmetric switching commonly exists in a network environment when a client/server network traffic flows, wherein clients are communicating with the server simultaneously. With this setup, the Server requires more bandwidth dedicated to the port where the server is connected; the reason for this is to avoid a bottleneck at the port.

Figure 2-6 Asymmetric switching

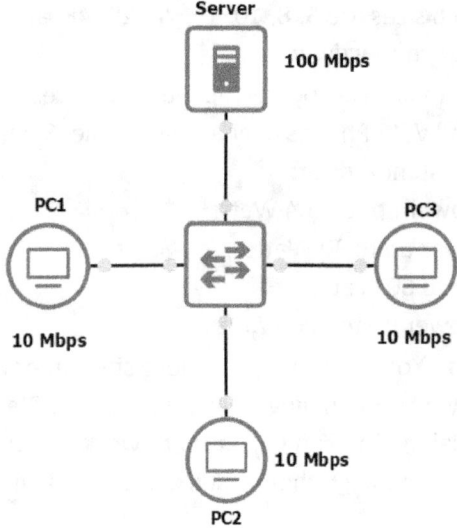

> **Terminologies:**
>
> *Bandwidth* – Rated throughput capacity of a given network medium or protocol, the maximum amount of data that travels across a medium.
> *Bottleneck* – Occurs when the path or link of a connection is smaller than needed.
> *Throughput* – The actual amount of data that travels across a medium successfully.
> (Source: *Cisco Certified Network Associate Study Guide, Todd Lamle*).

In Asymmetric switching, memory buffering is required to allow traffic from the 100 Mbps port to transmit to a 10 Mbps port without causing too much congestion at the smaller port. Memory buffering can be used to store and forward packets to the correct interface or port. Moreover, it can also be used when the destination port is not ready for any transaction. There are two common methods for memory buffer as stated below:

1. **Port-based** – frames are stored in the queue that is linked to a particular inbound interface. A frame is sent only if all the first frames from the queue are successfully transmitted. The concept is just like falling in line at a counter to pay for your grocery items.
2. **Shared Memory** – in this buffering, all incoming frames are placed into a common memory buffer shared by all ports on the switch until the outgoing port is ready to transmit. Memory allocation to a port is identified by how much is needed by each port. Switches dynamically allocate the shared memory in buffers to ports with high incoming traffic and do not give unnecessary buffers to idle or less-traffic ports. This process is called *Dynamic Allocation of Buffer Memory*. Frames that are in the buffer are dynamically linked (mapped) to the destination port. This allows the frame to be received on one port and transmitted on another port, without moving it into a different queue.

The switch maintains a map of frames to port links, giving the idea of where a packet should be transmitted. The switch clears out the map if the frames have been transmitted successfully. There is also a limitation on the number of frames in the buffer; it is restricted only to the size of the entire memory buffer since they are shared and not limited to one port. Furthermore, larger frames can be transmitted with fewer drops, which is very important in Asymmetric switching because of these limitations.

Switching Methods

Switching methods are the basis for the frame's latency on the switch. Following are the known switching modes.

Figure 2-7 Switching modes and their target bytes within a frame

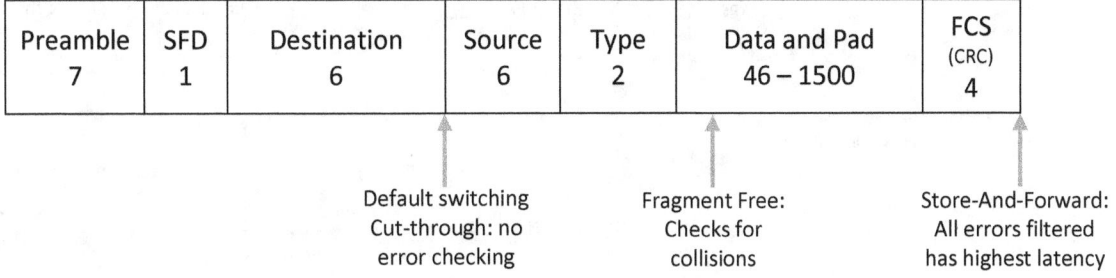

Store-and-Forward

The Primary switching method of Cisco. In this method, the entire frame is received before any forwarding is processed, and it copies the frame onto its onboard buffers and computes the Cyclic Redundancy Check (CRC). The latency occurs while the frame is being received. In larger frames, it takes more time to read its whole content, which has the highest latency. If the CRC is valid (not lower than 64 bytes and not greater than 1518 bytes, including CRC), the switch looks up the destination MAC address in its CAM table and determines the outbound interface. It then forwards the frame out to the correct port. Else, the frame is discarded. Cisco Catalyst 5000 series switches use this mode.

Figure 2-8 Store-and-Forward Switching

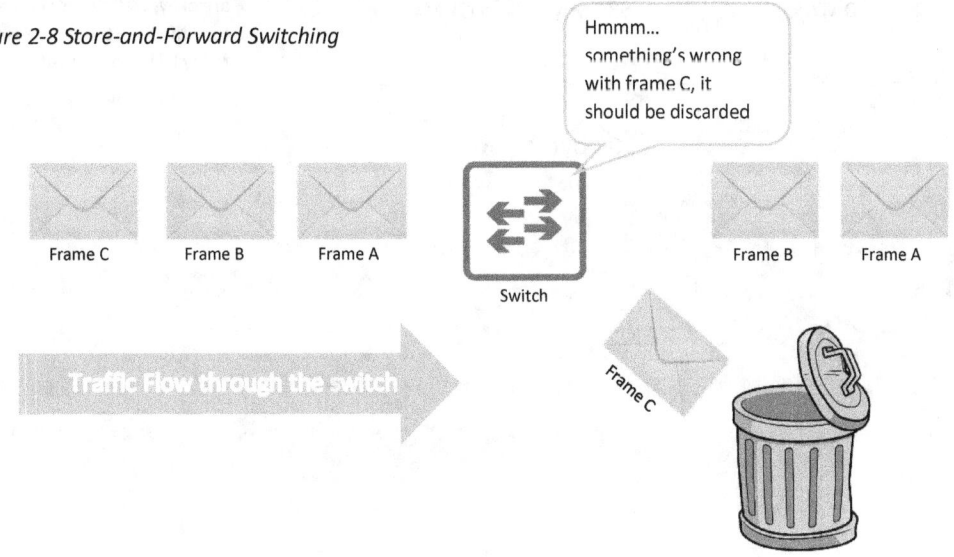

Cut-Through

- **Rapid Frame Forwarding** – Uses the FIFO algorithm. It offers the lowest level of latency since the switch does the forwarding as soon as it receives the Destination MAC address. Because this method skips the checking process (reading of CRC value in FCS), there are times that frames are relayed with errors. Common errors in a frame occur when a collision occurs, or the FCS doesn't match.

Figure 2-9 Rapid Frame Forwarding

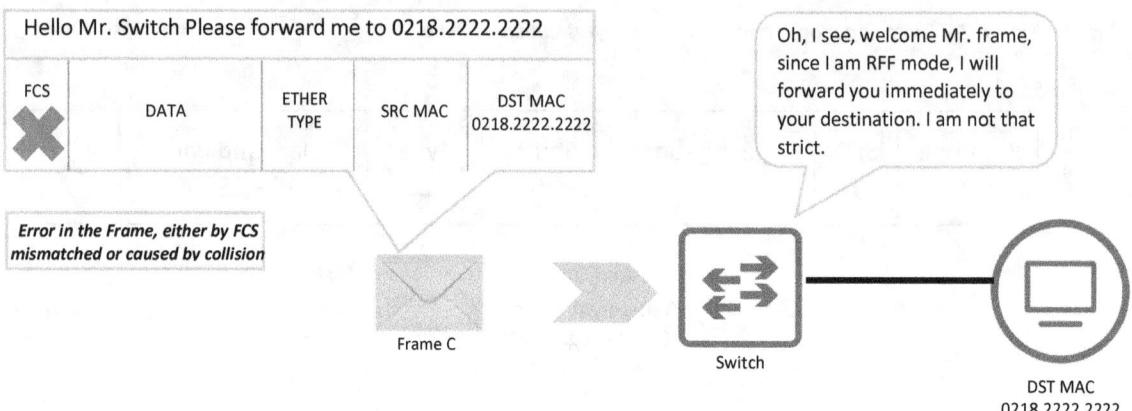

- **Fragment Free** – Is a modified version of cut-through switching wherein it starts to forward a frame after the first 64 bytes (collision window) are received and checked when no collision occurred on it, since most of the time, a collision occurs within the first 64 bytes. What it does is, look beyond just the destination, source MAC address, and ether type. What it examines is the 64 bytes in the frame. Because of its checking method, it has a medium level of latency. Below are the target bytes that the fragment free examines and the way how fragment free process the frame:

Figure 2-10 Fragment Free

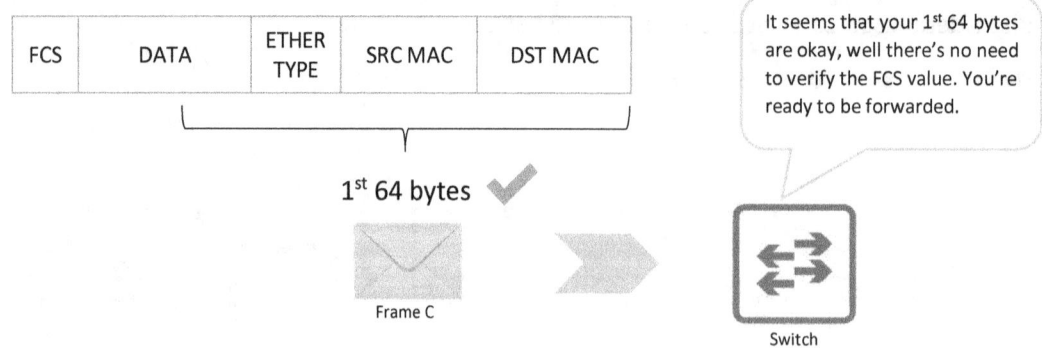

Basic Switch Management

CHAPTER 3

> **Terminologies:**
> *Cyclic Redundancy Check* – A methodology that detects errors, whereby the frame recipient makes a calculation by dividing the frame contents which a prime binary divisor and compares the remainder to a value stored in the frame by the sending code.
> *Collision window* – period of time where hosts checks if the medium is free and no other is transmitting.
> (Source: Cisco Certified Network Associate Study Guide, Todd Lamle).

Switching Boot Sequence

Like most of the devices, Cisco also has its Operating System. This operating system is what empowered the routers and switches of Cisco. The Cisco Internetwork Operating System (IOS) is the kernel of Cisco devices. It was created to deliver network services and enable networked applications, said Todd Lamle in his Book Cisco Certified Network Associate Study Guide written the year 2000.

The first time you power on a switch, a boot sequence occurs. It will run a *power-on self-test (POST)*, and if it passes successfully, the boot loader runs and initializes parts within the CPU, initializes the flash file, and then looks for and loads the Cisco IOS image. According to CCNA 6 curriculum, particularly in the CCNA-RS chapter 5, the Cisco IOS image can be defined within the boot environment variable. Next, if the variable is not set, an executable image file will be searched by the switch in the flash file system loading it into the RAM and launching it. Else, if the image itself is missing, the switch will prompt `switch:` where only limited commands are accepted to permit access to the Operating System files found in flash memory and files used to load or reload an OS.

If the OS is successfully loaded, it will look for a valid configuration called startup-config stored by default in Nonvolatile RAM (NVRAM), and it will initialize switches interfaces.

> **Terminology:**
> *Power on self-test (POST)* – A set of hardware diagnostics that runs on a hardware device when the device is powered on.
> (Source: Cisco Networking Academy Program: Second-Year Companion guide, Cisco Press.)

To set the BOOT environment variable, use the below command on a Cisco switch:

```
switch>en
switch#config t
switch(config)#boot system flash:/c2960-lanbasek9-mz.150-2.SE/c2960-lanbasek9-mz.150.-2.SE.bin
```

Where in:

Switch Recovery from System Crash

What happens if there is a system crash? So, the best way to resolve the problem is to make a recovery on the switch. To make a recovery, the boot loader should be accessed. A boot loader is accessed through a console connection to the switch. Here are the steps to access the boot loader:

1. Connect PC to the switch through the console port using console cable.
2. Run a terminal application to open the Command-line Interface of the switch and configure the correct baud rate. Usually, cisco device is at a 9600n baud rate.
3. Unplug the power cord of the switch.
4. Plug again the power cord and, at the same time or within 15 seconds, press and hold the MODE button on the front of the switch until the System LED indicator turns to an amber color and then turns solid green.

The boot loader will display on the terminal application or emulator when the steps above are followed properly. Instead of `switch>`, it will be displayed as a `switch:` indicating that you are now in the boot loader command prompt.

Available commands through the boot loader are limited. To display the list of available commands, you can use the **help** command.

Figure 3-1 Boot loader

```
switch: dir flash:
Directory of flash:/

    2  -rwx      11607161    Mar 1 2013 03:10:47 +00:00  c2960-lanbasek9-mz.150-2.SE.bin
    3  -rwx          1809    Mar 1 2013 00:02:48 +00:00  config.text
    5  -rwx          1919    Mar 1 2013 00:02:48 +00:00  private-config.text
    6  -rwx         59416    Mar 1 2013 00:02:49 +00:00  multiple-fs

32514048 bytes total (20841472 bytes free)
```

(Image: Courtesy of Cisco Networking Academy Program)

Switch LED Indicators

Switch LED indicators are visual indicators to help Network Administrators or any IT technician analyze the switch's current status. There are two common types of LED indicators in a Cisco Switch.

Command
Storage Device
Path to location in file system
Filename of the image

- Green – Link is Active

1. **System LED** – Shows if the switch is powered on or not.
2. **Port LED States:**
   - Off – no link or shutdown

- Blinking Green – Data activity
- Alternating Green and Amber – Link Fault
- Amber – no data is sent; usually happens when the switch is first powered on
- Blinking Amber – Port is in blocking state, preventing switching loop.

(Image: Courtesy of Cisco Networking Academy Program)

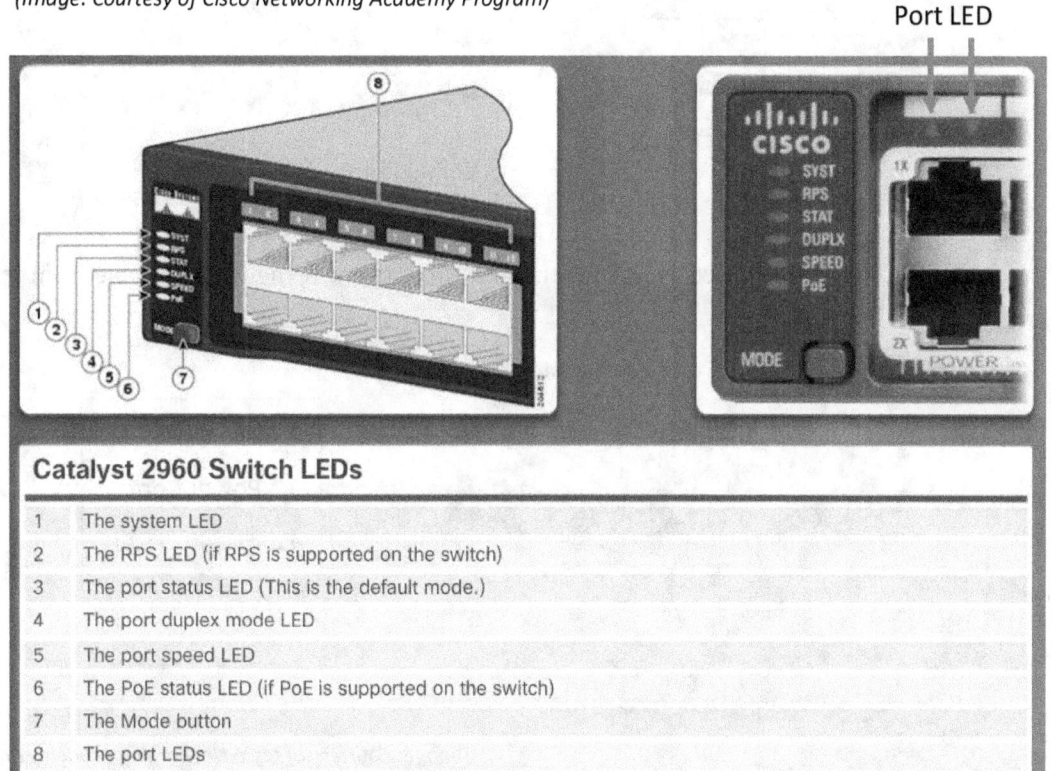

Catalyst 2960 Switch LEDs

1	The system LED
2	The RPS LED (if RPS is supported on the switch)
3	The port status LED (This is the default mode.)
4	The port duplex mode LED
5	The port speed LED
6	The PoE status LED (if PoE is supported on the switch)
7	The Mode button
8	The port LEDs

Switch Basic Configuration

Initial Step

The way how we configure a switch is the same approach in configuring a router. We need to access the switch's console port and use a terminal application or emulator to access the Command-Line Interface. Rollover types of cable can also be used to access the switch configuration terminal. *(Steps are shown in the following pages).*

Figure 3-3 Examples of Terminal Applications

Figure 3-4 Examples of Console and Rollover Cable

1. To access a Cisco switch for the first time, connect the console cable from the PC to the switch.

Figure 3-5 PC connected to switch using console cable

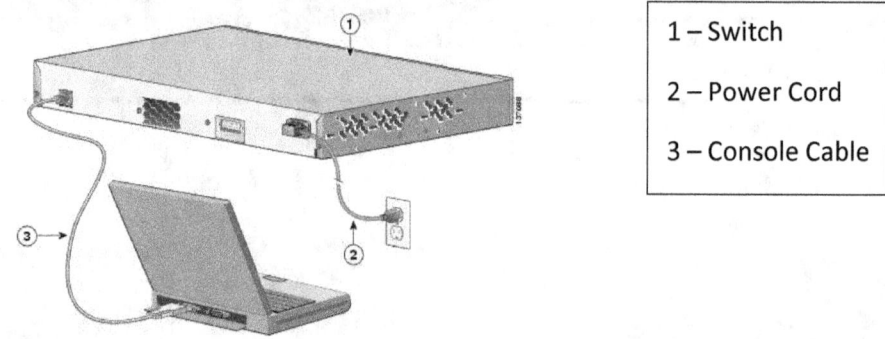

1 – Switch

2 – Power Cord

3 – Console Cable

(Image: Courtesy of Cisco Networking Academy Program)

2. Next is to open a terminal emulator; in this case, Putty is used. Needed fields for Putty are the Serial line name, the Speed or Baud rate, and of course, the Serial option should be selected.

Figure 3-6 Putty Interface

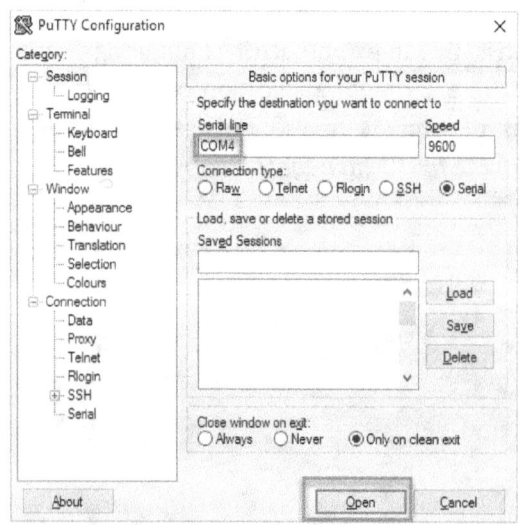

3. The name of the Serial line depends on every PC. If you are not sure about the name, access the device manager in Windows. Press Windows button + R (Windows Run) and enter 'devmgmt.msc' on the key board.

Figure 3-7 Run Device Manager

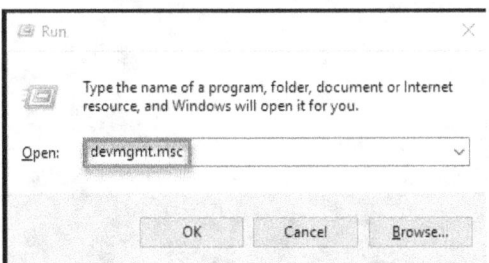

4. On the Device Manager, look for Ports (COM & LPT); there, you can verify the name of your serial connection.

Figure 3-8 Device Manager

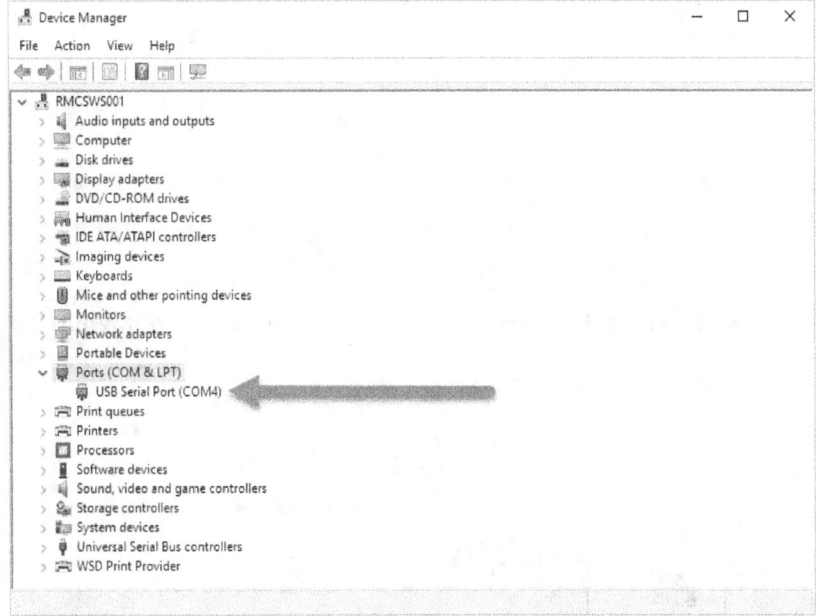

5. Not following the above image, let us say that the Serial Line name is COM1

Figure 3-9 Putty Interface

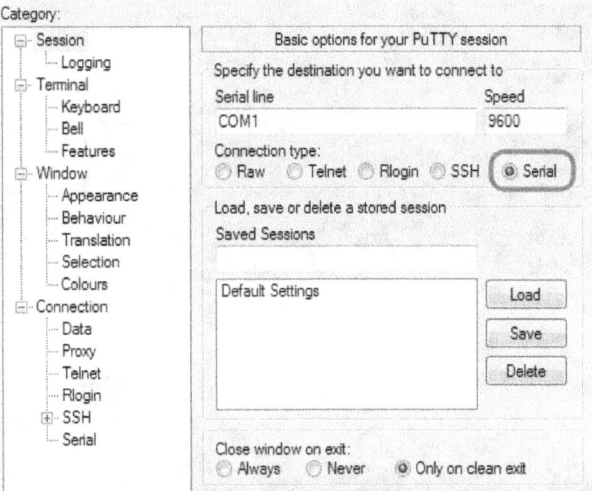

6. On the putty interface, select serial under the list of connections

Figure 3-10 Putty Interface, Serial Navigation Field

7. It will open the Options controlling local serial lines page.

Figure 3-11 Putty Interface: Options controlling local serial lines

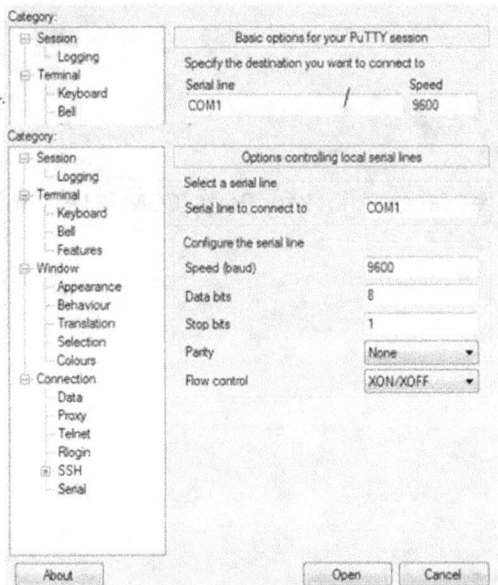

8. Enter the serial line name in the *Serial line to connect to* textbox.

Figure 3-12 Putty Interface: Serial Line to connect to

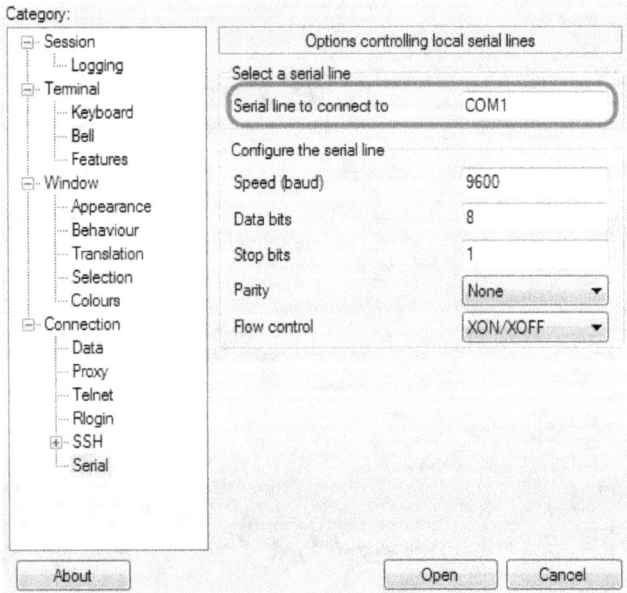

9. In the Speed or baud rate, for the 2960 series, enter 9600. For 300 and 500 series managed switches, set the baud rate to 115200. For data bits and bits, the recommended value is **1**, no need to change the value. For Parity, set it to **None**.

Figure 3-13 Putty Interface: Speed (baud), Data and Stop bits, Parity

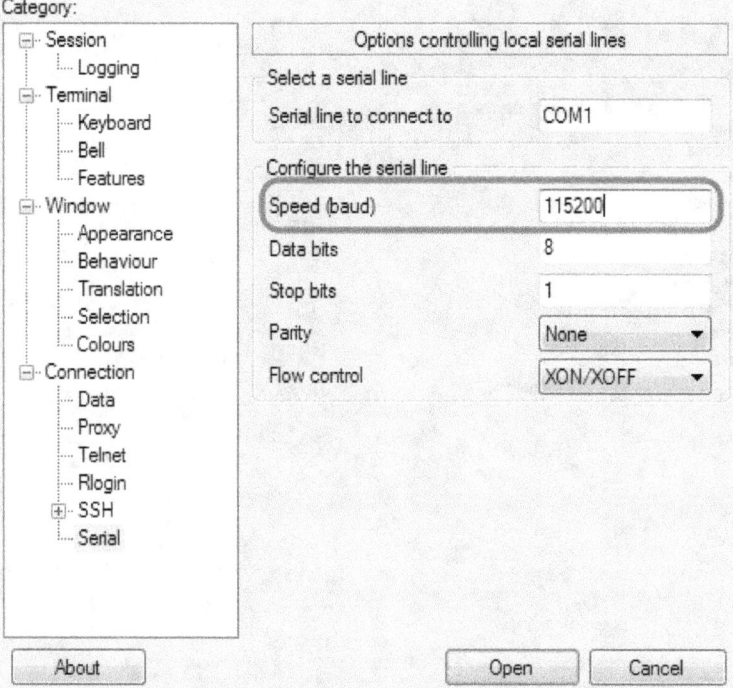

10. For flow control drop down menu, **none** is recommended

Figure 3-14 Putty Interface: Flow control

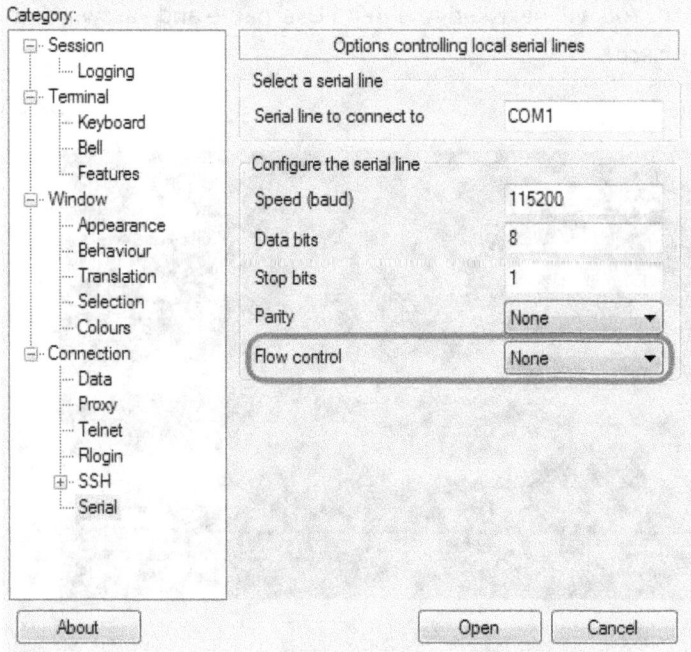

27

11.   *This is optional*; if you want to save the connection setting for future use, go to **Session** located at the upper left side of the display.

12. If everything is set, click open

Figure 3-15 Putty Interface

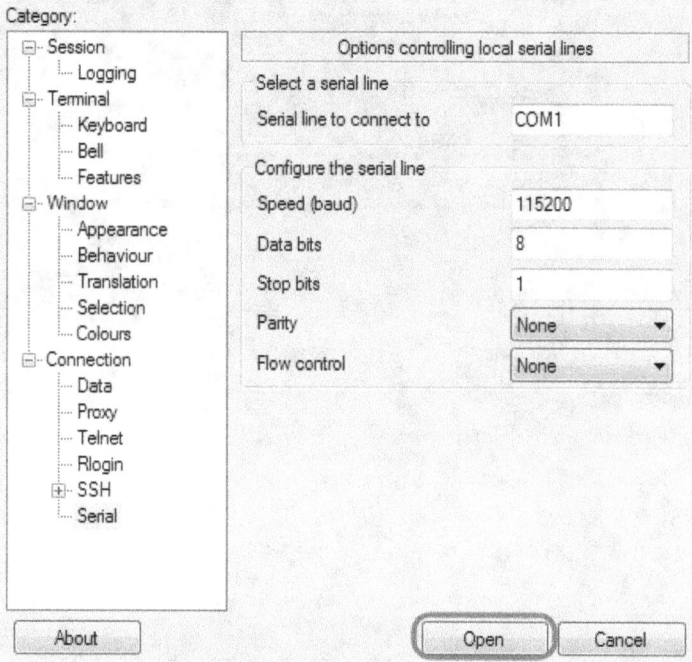

13. The Putty Console window opens. To activate the Command line, hit **Enter** on the keyboard. You will be asked to enter a Username and Password; the default value for these is **cisco.**

Figure 3-16 Putty CLI interface

Remote Access

It is not all the time that you are near to the switch. It is a good practice in network management to set a virtual interface where you can assign an address to access your device even if you are far away. The concept of remote access is you will be able to access your devices even you are not directly connected on the device provided you are still part or connected to the network. This allows you to still manage your network without moving to another physical location to check or configure the device.

To configure a switch remotely, the switch must be configured with an IP Address, subnet mask, and default gateway. There is one particular Switch Virtual Interface (SVI) used to manage the switch. By default, it is managed and controlled through VLAN 1, which is the management VLAN. For security purposes, it is recommended to use VLAN 1 as your management access.

Figure 3-17 Sample Network Topology where switches are placed in different areas.

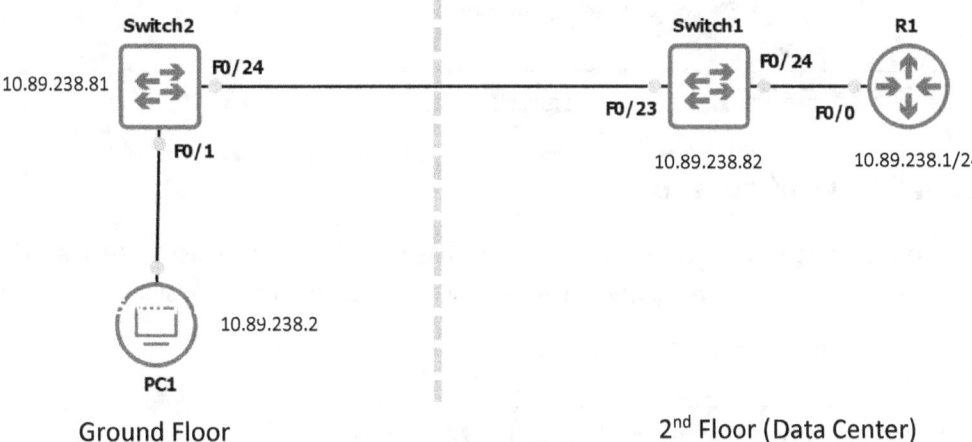

Ground Floor   2nd Floor (Data Center)

Figure 3-17 shows how PC1 accesses Switch 1 even not directly connected to it. Through remote access, PC1 can still configure the device by using any terminal emulator or even in CMD by just entering the telnet command and by declaring the IP address of the Switch 1.

Refer to figure 3-18 when using putty. You may access the switch remotely through Putty either by **telnet** connection or **ssh** connection.

Figure 3-18 Putty Interface using telnet connections

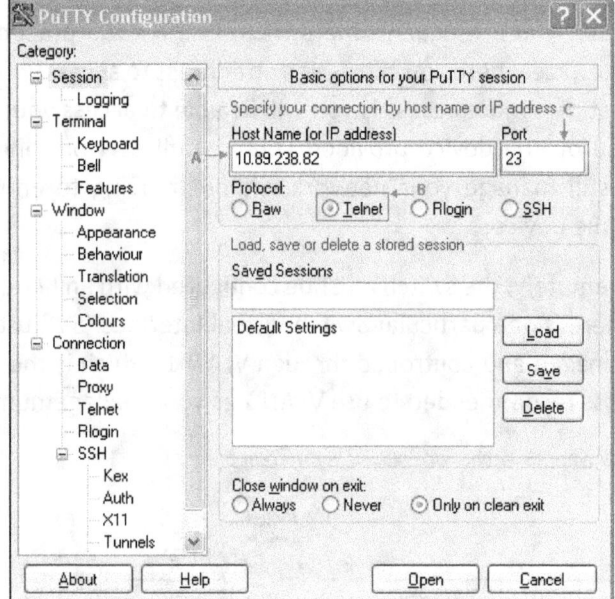

A – IP Address of Switch 1

B – Telnet Connection

C – Port number of Telnet

Basic Switch Configuration

You can't do remote access if your switch has no IP Address. To assign IP in a switch, it is important to identify the address space available in the network. Let us consider the below figure.

Figure 3-19 Simple network topology

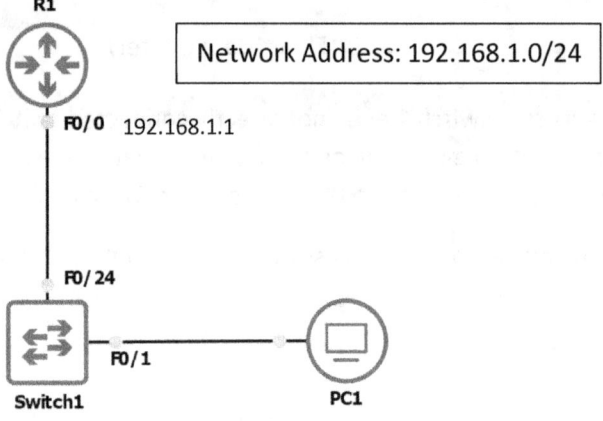

VLAN1: 192.168.1.254

The basic rule in assigning IP to a switch is that the switch will get the last usable IP address of the network. From the example in figure 1-19, we have a network address of 192.168.1.0/24. This specific network address has 256 IP addresses and 254 usable IP addresses assigned to any network device or host. So, if we try to examine the last usable IP address from that given network, it is 192.168.1.254.

Take note that if there is a second switch, therefore, it will have the second to the last usable IP address, when based from the above network address, it is 192.168.1.253.

To assign an IP address in a switch we used the following commands. (We will base the configuration on the topology given in Figures 1-19.

Setting Host Name, IP Address, and Default Gateway

`switch>`**`en`**	Moves the user from user mode to privileged mode. (short for '`enable`')
`switch#`**`config t`**	Moves to global configuration mode
`switch(config)#`**`hostname Switch1`**	Setting a local hostname of the switch
`Switch1(config)#`**`int VLAN1`**	Enters the switch virtual interface (SVI) for VLAN 1
`Switch1(config-if)#`**`ip add 192.168.1.254 255.255.255.0`**	Assigns IP Address of 192.168.1.254 to switch with a subnet mask of 255.255.255.0 in VLAN 1 for remote access
`Switch1(config-if)#`**`no shut`**	Turns the interface on (short for '`no shutdown`')
`Switch1(config-if)#`**`exit`**	Returns to global configuration mode
`Switch1(config)#`**`ip default-gateway 192.168.1.1`**	Configure default gateway for the switch (Default Gateway is the IP Address of the Router)
`Switch1(config)#`**`end`**	Returns to privileged mode
`Switch1#`**`copy run start`**	Saves the running configuration to the startup config (short for '`copy running-config startup-config`')

Some commands might help manage your switch; the following are some of the known commands:

Resetting Switch Configuration

`switch#`**`delete flash:VLAN.dat`**	Removes the VLAN database from the flash memory
`Delete filename [VLAN.dat]?`	Press **'Enter'**
`Delete flash:VLAN.dat? [confirm]`	Press **'Enter'** to reconfirm
`switch#`**`erase startup-config`**	Will erase the file from NVRAM
`<output omitted>`	
`Switch#`**`reload`**	Restarts the Switch

Setting Interface Description

`switch(config)#`**`int f0/24`**	Enters interface configuration mode
`switch(config-if)#`**`description Connection to Router`**	Adds a label or description of the interface. It is only significant locally.

`switch(config)#int f0/24`	Enters interface configuration mode
`switch(config-if)#mdix auto`	Enables Auto-MDIX on the interface
`switch(config-if)#no mdix auto`	Disables Auto-MDIX on the interface

Setting Duplex Operation

`switch(config)#int f0/24`	Enters interface configuration mode
Options Below (Choose only one)	
`switch(config-if)#duplex full`	Forces full-duplex operation
`switch(config-if)#duplex auto`	Enables auto-duplex configuration
`switch(config-if)#duplex half`	Forces half-duplex operation

Setting Operation Speed

`switch(config)#int f0/24`	Enters interface configuration mode
Options Below (Choose only one)	
`switch(config-if)#speed 10`	Forces interface to 10 Mbps operation
`switch(config-if)#speed 100`	Forces interface to 100 Mbps operation
`switch(config-if)#speed auto`	Enables auto speed configuration

The MDIX auto Command

By default, in a cisco environment, there is a specific type of cable recommended for every connection. For example, when connecting to Servers or PCs, we use the straight-through type of cable, while when establishing a link for switch to another switch, we use crossover cables. This recommendation of cables is made by the switch automatically through detecting the type of medium used.

Enabling the Medium-Dependent Interface Crossover (Auto-MDIX) will allow you to use any type of cable and automatically set the interfaces to correct for incorrect cabling.

> **Note:**
> *Auto-MDIX is enabled by default on Cisco IOS with release versions of 12.2(18) SE or Later. For Cisco IOS release 12.1(14) EA1 and 12.2(18)SE, Auto-MDIX is disabled by default. If you are configuring Cisco devices where Auto-MDIX is enabled, the command doesn't show up. Setting the interfaces to Auto-MDIX must the interfaces be set to Speed Auto and Duplex Auto so that the feature operates correctly.*
> *(Source: CCNA Routing and Switching Portable Command Guide, Scott Empson)*

The Table below shows the different link-state results from Auto-MDIX settings with correct and incorrect cabling. *(Source: CCNA Routing and Switching Portable Command Guide, Scott Empson)*

Figure 3-20 Link state result from Auto-MDIX

Local Side Auto-MDIX	Remote Side Auto-MDIX	With Correct Cabling	With Incorrect Cabling
On	On	Link up	Link up
On	Off	Link up	Link up
Off	On	Link up	Link up
Off	Off	Link up	Link down

Verifying Configurations

Every network administrator or IT technician assigned in the network management must know how to check and verify configurations entered on the device. Verifying the configuration on the switch is done but depends on the type of configuration that requires confirmation or checking. Below are some of the basic commands to verify configurations.

`switch#`**`show version`**	Display System Hardware and Software Status
`switch#`**`show flash`**	Display information about flash file system
`switch#`**`show mac address-table`** OR `switch#`**`show mac-address-table`**	Display the CAM table
`switch#`**`show running-config`** OR `switch#`**`show run`**	Display current operating configurations in DRAM
`switch#`**`Show startup-config`**	Display the current startup configurations in NVRAM
`switch#`**`show history`**	Display the history of commands entered
`switch#`**`show interfaces`** `[interface_id]`	Display Interface status and configuration
`switch#`**`show ip`** `[interface_id]`	Display IP information of an Interface
`switch#`**`show controllers ethernet`** `[interface_id]` **`phy	include Auto-MDIX`**	Verify auto-MDIX settings
`Switch#`**`show cdp neighbor`**	Display neighboring devices' information that are connected to the current device

Here is an example of the display when using show run. Most of the time, a show run is used to check the device's status and its connection.

Figure 3-21 Result of show run config

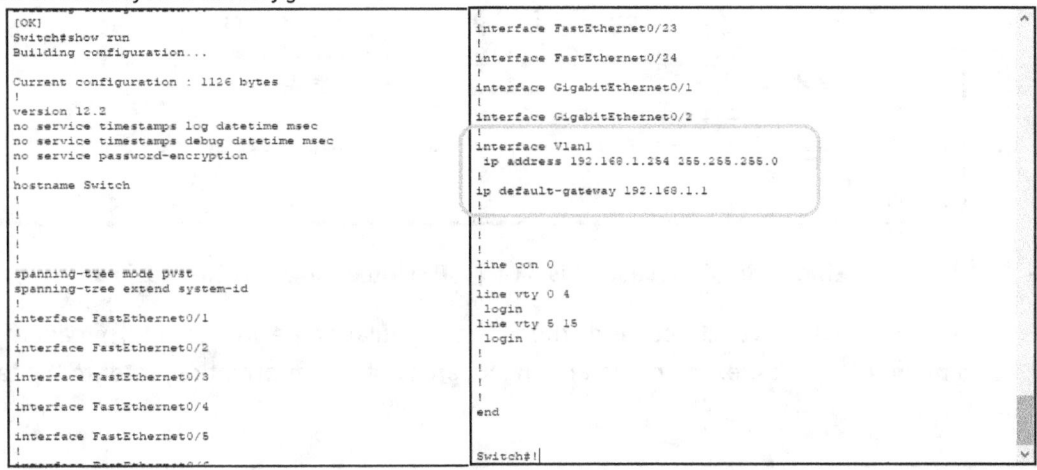

Network Access Layer Issues

Another way of verifying links is by using the `show interface` command. Using this command, we can check if the connection for layer 1 and Layer 2 is active. For this example, we will be using the previous topology in Figure 3-19.

Figure 3-22 Result of Show Interface

```
                         A              B
Switch#show interface f0/24
FastEthernet0/24 is up, line protocol is up (connected)
  Hardware is Lance, address is 0090.2122.7c18 (bia 0090.2122.7c18)
 BW 100000 Kbit, DLY 1000 usec,
     reliability 255/255, txload 1/255, rxload 1/255
  Encapsulation ARPA, loopback not set
  Keepalive set (10 sec)
  Full-duplex, 100Mb/s
  input flow-control is off, output flow-control is off
  ARP type: ARPA, ARP Timeout 04:00:00
  Last input 00:00:08, output 00:00:05, output hang never
  Last clearing of "show interface" counters never
  Input queue: 0/75/0/0 (size/max/drops/flushes); Total output drops: 0

  Queueing strategy: fifo
  Output queue :0/40 (size/max)
  5 minute input rate 0 bits/sec, 0 packets/sec
  5 minute output rate 0 bits/sec, 0 packets/sec
     956 packets input, 193351 bytes, 0 no buffer
     Received 956 broadcasts, 0 runts, 0 giants, 0 throttles
     0 input errors, 0 CRC, 0 frame, 0 overrun, 0 ignored, 0 abort
     0 watchdog, 0 multicast, 0 pause input
     0 input packets with dribble condition detected
     2357 packets output, 263570 bytes, 0 underruns
     0 output errors, 0 collisions, 10 interface resets
     0 babbles, 0 late collision, 0 deferred
     0 lost carrier, 0 no carrier
     0 output buffer failures, 0 output buffers swapped out

Switch#!
```

A – Indicating that Layer 1 is ok | B – Indicating that Layer 2 is ok

The details enclosed inside the red-rectangular shape are the determinants if there occurs a network layer issue. To understand the meaning of this information, refer to the table below.

Figure 3-23 Error Types

Error Type	Description
Input Errors	Total number of errors. Including runts, giants, no buffer, CRC frame, overrun, and ignored counts
Runts	Smaller packets than the minimum packet size required in a medium which are then discarded. Any Ethernet packet lower than 64 bytes is considered as a runt.
Giants	Packets that exceeded the max packet size which are then discarded. Any Ethernet packet that is higher than 1518 bytes is considered as a giant.
CRC	Created when the calculated checksum is not the same with the checksum received.
Output Errors	Sum of all errors that disallowed the final transmission of datagrams out of the interface that is being inspected.
Collisions	Refers to the number of messages that are retransmitted due to Ethernet collisions
Late Collisions	The collision that happens after the 512 bits of the frame have been transmitted.

Troubleshooting process

Below is a flow chart representation of how should an individual deal with Switch Media Issues.

Figure 3-24 A Flowchart of Troubleshooting process

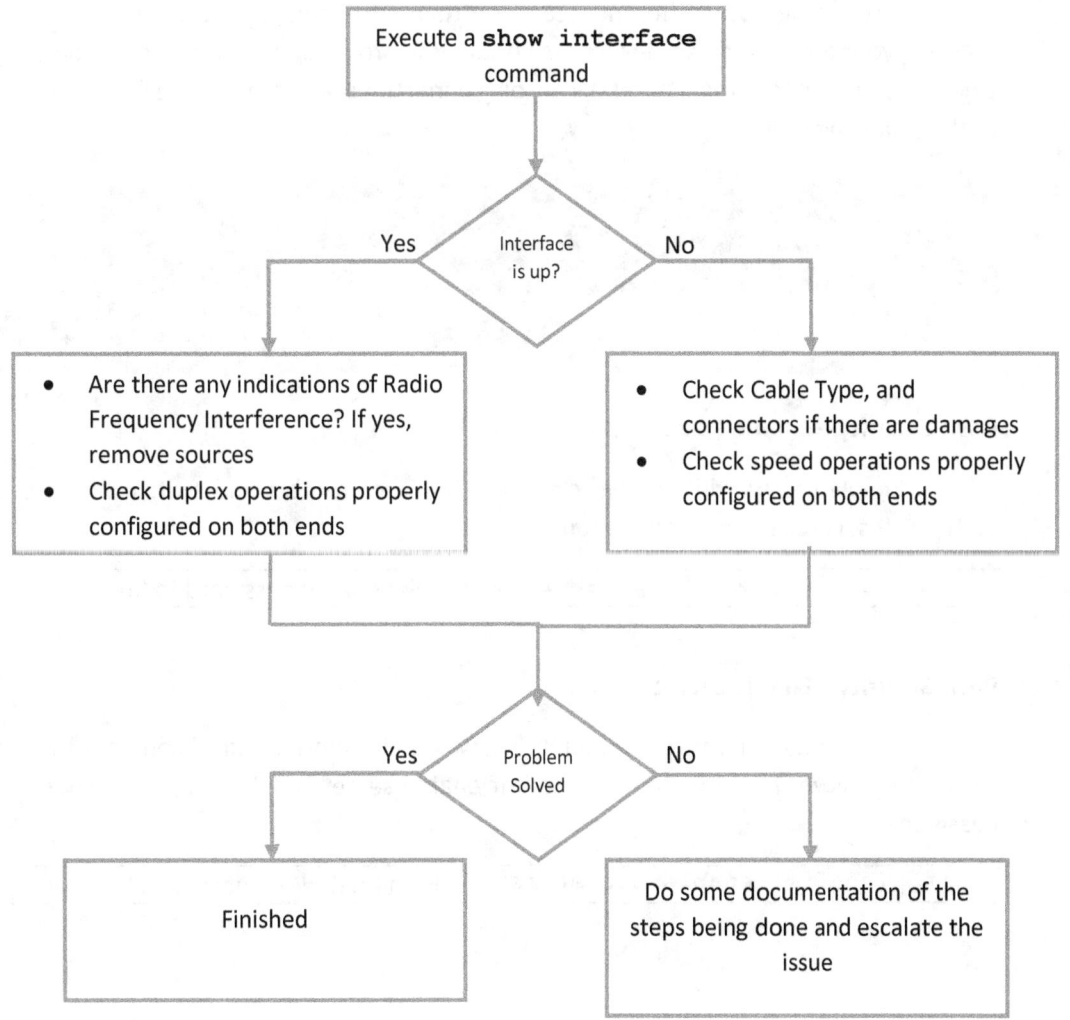

> **Note:**
> *Radio Frequency Interference (RFI) – Also known as Electromagnetic Interference (EMI), is a disturbance generated by an external source that affects an electrical circuit by electromagnetic induction, electrostatic coupling, or conduction.*
> *(Source: https://en.m.wikipedia.org)*

Switch Security

Various security measures can be done on a switch. Some of these will be discussed in this section.

Setting Passwords

It is important to have your network devices be secured in a network, especially when remote access is possible. Remember, when an intruder receives unauthorized access to one of your devices, this could bring bigger problems. The intruder will have full admin access, and the worst is, the attacker may change some of the configurations and destroy the setup of your network. If this happens, you are no longer the Network Administrator.

Cisco comes with different access control in protecting the switches. The basic means of securing your device is by setting a password. Password setting on a switch can be done through Line vty (common to remote access), console connections, and ssh. For the list of commands, refer to the following table.

> **Note:**
> *SSH – Stands for Secure Shell, is a cryptographic network protocol for operating network services securely over an unsecured network. Commonly used for remote access.*
> *(Source: https://en.m.wikipedia.org)*

Basic Security – Enable Password

Enable password is the basic security for Cisco routers and switches on pre-10.3 older systems. It secures the privileged mode.

Command	Description
`switch(config)#enable password msu`	Set enable password to 'msu'

Basic Security – Enable Secret

It is the newer version of enable password and more secured compared to the old one since the password is already encrypted. If enable secret is activated, it overrides the enable password.

Command	Description
`switch(config)#enable secret msu`	Set enable secret to 'msu'

Line Commands - Console

Line commands are used to secure the devices in the User mode level. Use the following commands to secure the console access.

`switch(config)#`**`line con 0`**	Enters line console mode, zero means single console port
`switch(config-line)#`**`password msu`**	Sets the password to 'msu'
`switch(config-line)#`**`login`**	Enables password checking

Line Commands – vty

It is used to set a password for telnet connections at the User mode level, especially for remote access. For the non-enterprise edition of Cisco IOS, line vty is limited to only 5 lines, which means 0 to 4.

`switch(config)#`**`line vty 0 4`**	Enters vty line mode for all five lines
`switch(config-line)#`**`password msu`**	Sets the password to 'msu'
`switch(config-line)#`**`login`**	Enables password checking

Password Encryption

By default, only enable secret stays encrypted, and all other security measures discussed earlier stay unencrypted. With this, line passwords are visible when someone issues a show run command in the CLI. Refer to the below figure to verify.

Figure 3-25 Enable password and line commands not encrypted

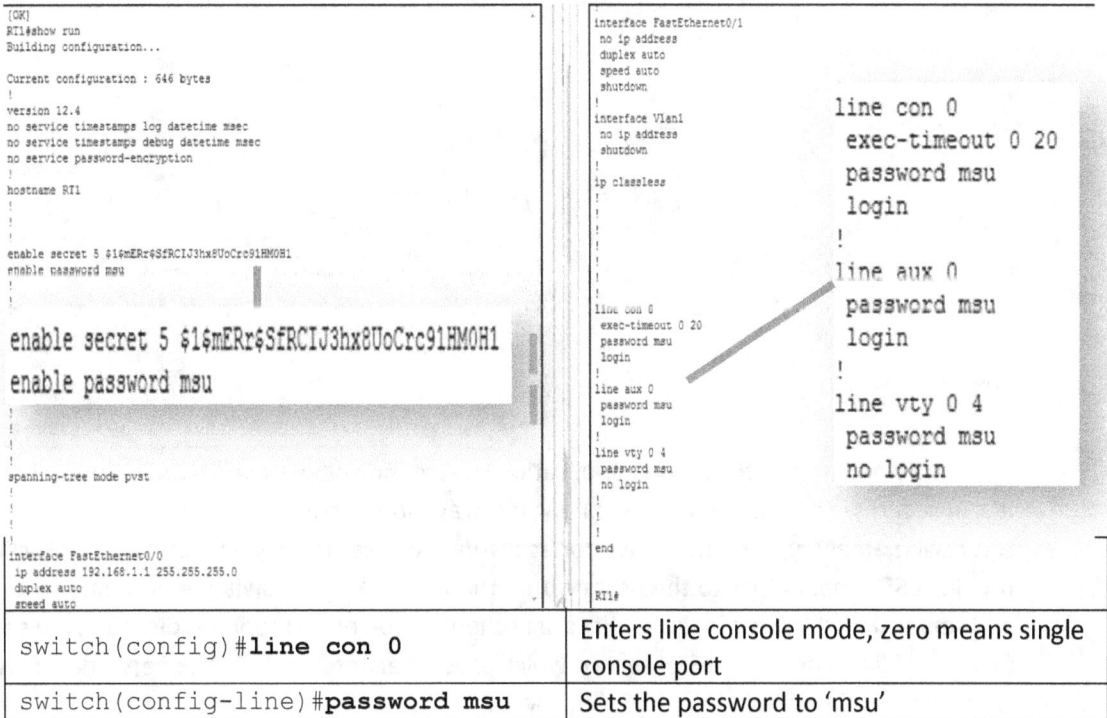

`switch(config)#`**`line con 0`**	Enters line console mode, zero means single console port
`switch(config-line)#`**`password msu`**	Sets the password to 'msu'

`switch(config-line)#`**`login`**	Enables password checking
`switch(config)#`**`line vty 0 4`**	Enters vty line mode for all five lines
`switch(config-line)#`**`password msu`**	Sets the password to 'msu'
`switch(config-line)#`**`login`**	Enables password checking
`switch(config)#`**`no service password-encryption`**	Turns off password encryption

Note:

If you have turned on service password-encryption, used it, and then turned it off, any passwords that you have entered between the lines remains encrypted. While new passwords not included in the line remains unencrypted.
(Source: CCNA Routing and Switching Portable Command Guide, Scott Empson)

Observe how the service password encryption hides the passwords; refer to figure 3-26.
(Note: Please disregard aux, this is an image taken from a router, password encryption to switch is the same with router)

Figure 3-26 Service password encryption taking in effect

```
Building configuration...

Current configuration : 671 bytes
!
version 12.4
no service timestamps log datetime msec
no service timestamps debug datetime msec
no service password-encryption
!
hostname RT1
!
!
!
enable secret 5 $1$mERr$SfPCIJ3hx8UoCrc91HM0H1
enable password 7 082C5F5B
!
!
!
!
!
!
!
!
!
!
spanning-tree mode pvst
!
!
!
!
interface FastEthernet0/0
 ip address 192.168.1.1 255.255.255.0
 duplex auto
 speed auto

 no ip address
 duplex auto
 speed auto
 shutdown
!
interface Vlan1
 no ip address
 shutdown
!
ip classless
!
!
!
!
!
!
line con 0
 exec-timeout 0 20
 password 7 082C5F5B
 login
!
line aux 0
 password 7 082C5F5B
 login
!
line vty 0 4
 password 7 082C5F5B
 login
!
!
!
end

RT1#
```

Telnet may be the default application in accessing devices, but the disadvantage of this is it is unsecured. To access devices securely, it is way more recommended to use Secure Shell (SSH) to provide an encrypted alternative for accessing devices. The switch acts as an SSH client that provides SSH capabilities to the users within the network in the switch environment. It uses an SSH server that will provide the services. If authentication of SSH server is disabled, the switch will take any reliable or trusted SSH server, which causes security issues in the network. If SSH service is enabled on the switch, security is improved.

Note: The information below will be based on the Cisco Catalyst 2960-X switches with IOS release 15.0(2)EX.

Prerequisites

There are some prerequisites for configuring Secure shell; refer to the following bullets as enumerated from www.cisco.com:

- A switch needs a Rivest, Shamir, and Adleman (RSA) public/Private key pair for the SSH to work. This is the same with Secure Copy Protocol (SCP), which relies on SSH for its secure transport
- SSH, authentication, and authorization on the switch must be configured correctly first before enabling SCP
- Because SCP relies on SSH for secure transport, RSA key pair must be in the Router
- SCP relies on SSH for security
- The SCP requires authentication, authorization, and accounting (AAA) authorization to be configured so the router can determine whether the user has the correct privilege level.
- To use SCP, a user must have correct authorization; with this, the user can use SCP to copy any file in the Cisco IOS File System (IFS) to and from a switch by using the **copy** command. An authorized administrator can also do this from a workstation.
- Configure a Hostname and Domain name in the device.

Restrictions

Below are the restrictions when configuring SSH in a switch (Cisco 2960-X IOS Release 15.0(2)EX) basing on the cisco netacad teachings (Source www.cisco.com):

- The switch must support RSA
- SSH supports only the execution-shell application
- The SSH server and the SSH client are supported only on Data Encryption Standard (DES) (56-bit) and 3DES (168-bit) data encryption software. In DES software images, DES is the only encryption algorithm available. In 3DES software images, both DES and 3DES encryption algorithms are available
- The switch supports the Advanced Encryption Standard (AES) encryption algorithm with a 128-bit key, 192-bit key, or 256-bit key. However, symmetric cipher AES to encrypt the keys is not supported.
- The software does not support IPSec.
- When using SCP, you can't enter the password into the **copy** command. You must enter the password when prompted.
- The login banner is not supported in Secure Shell version 1, only in version 2.
- The -l keyword and userid :{number} {ip-address} delimiter and arguments are mandatory when configuring the alternative method of Reverse SSH for console access.

Guideline in configuring SSH in a Switch

Follow the following guidelines when configuring the switch as an SSH Server or SSH client (Source: www.cisco.com):

- An SSHv2 server and the reverse can use an RSA key pair generated by an SSHv1 server.
- If the SSH server is running on a stack master and the stack master fails, the new stack master uses the RSA key pair generated by the previous stack master.
- If you get CLI error messages after entering the **crypto key, generate rsa** global configuration command, and RSA key pair has not been generated. Reconfigure the hostname and domain, and then enter the **crypto key generate rsa** command.
- When generating rsa key pair, the message No host name specified might appear. If it does, you must configure an IP domain name using the **ip domain-name** global configuration command.
- When configuring the local authentication and authorization authentication method, make sure that AAA is disabled on the console.

Secure Copy Protocol

Basing on cisco.com, Secure Copy Protocol or SCP provides a secure and authenticated method for copying switch configurations or switch image files. The behavior of SCP is similar to that of remote copy (rcp), which comes from the Berkeley r-tools suite, except that SCP relies on SSH for security. SCP also requires that authentication, authorization, and accounting (AAA) authorization be configured so the switch can determine whether the user has the correct privilege level.

> **Note:**
> It is recommended to use SSH version 2 since there are security issues in SSH version 1. To configure SSH, it is recommended to change the username of the device and will not use the default. The implementation of SSH requires Cisco IOS software to support Rivest, Shamir, Adleman (RSA) Authentication and minimum Data Encryption Standard (DES) encryption (A cryptographic software image) (Source: CCNA Routing and Switching Portable Command Guide, Scott Empson)

> **Note:**
> The Cisco IOS image used must be a k9(crypto) image in order to support SSH. For example, c3750e-universalk9-tar.122-35.SE5.tar is a k9 (crypto) image
>
> (Source: www.cisco.com)

To make SSH working, an IP must be configured on the management VLAN interface, which will be used as the address to be accessed using SSH.

`switch(config)#`**`hostname msu`**	Set hostname to msu
`msu(config-if)#`**`int VLAN1`**	Open management VLAN
`msu(config-if)#`**`ip add 192.168.1.254 255.255.255.0`**	Assigns IP Address of 192.168.1.254 to switch with a subnet mask of 255.255.255.0 in VLAN 1 for remote access
`msu(config-if)#`**`no shut`**	Turns on the interface VLAN1

`msu(config-if)#`**`exit`**		Return to global configuration mode
`msu(config)#`**`ip default-gateway 192.168.1.1`**		Configure default gateway for the switch (Default Gateway is the IP Address of the Router)
Options Below (Choose only one)		
Option1	`msu(config)#`**`username msu password sulu`**	Creates a local credential with username msu and password sulu
Option2	`msu(config)#`**`username msu privilege 15 secret sulu`**	Creates a local credential with username msu and secret sulu
`msu(config)#`**`ip domain-name msu.sulu`**		Creates a host domain for the switch
`msu(config)#`**`crypto key generate rsa`**		Enables the SSH server for local and remote authentication on the switch and generates an RSA key pair. Generating an RSA key pair for the switch automatically enables SSH
When you generate rsa keys, you are required to enter a modulus length. The longer it is, the more it is secured but it takes longer to generate and to use. It is recommended to use a minimum size of 1024 bits.		

```
msu(config)#crypto key generate rsa
The name for the keys will be: msu.msu.sulu
Choose the size of the key modulus in the range of 360 to 2048 for
your
  General Purpose Keys. Choosing a key modulus greater than 512 may
take
  a few minutes.

How many bits in the modulus [512]: 1024
% Generating 1024 bit RSA keys, keys will be non-exportable...[OK]
```

Cont. To configure the SSH Sever on a switch, the following configuration is required.	
`msu(config)#`**`ip ssh version 2`**	Enables SSH version on the switch
`msu(config)#`**`ip ssh time-out 90`**	Enter time-out value in seconds. The default is 120. Range is 0 -120. This is applied during the SSH negotiation phase; after the connection, the switch uses the default time-out values of the CLI-based sessions. By default, only five simultaneous encrypted SSH connections for multiple CLI-based sessions over the network are available (Session 0 to 4). After the execution shell starts, the CLIE-based session time-out value returns to the default of 10 minutes
`msu(config)#`**`ip ssh authentication-retries 2`**	Set the number of times that a client can re-authenticate to the server. The default is 3; the range is 0 to 5. After the declared number, the session will be cut off.
`msu(config)#`**`line vty 0 10`**	Moves to vty line configuration for all 11 lines of the switch

`msu(config-line)#login local`	Enables password checking on a per-user basis according to the credential created on the global configuration mode.
`msu(config-line)#transport input ssh`	Limits remote connectivity to SSH connections only, and it disables telnet.

To verify SSH, use the following commands

`msu#show ip ssh`	Verifies that SSH is enabled
`msu#show ssh`	Checks the SSH connection to the device

Restricting Virtual Terminal Access to selected users.

Additional security improvements when using SSH is you only select trusted devices from your network that have the privilege to access the device. To do this, you must create an Access-list rule (ACL) in a standard format allowing only desired users to access the switch.

	To allow single user, use the below command	
Option1	`msu(config)#access-list 2 permit host 192.168.1.2`	Permits the host with an of 192.168.1.2
	To allow multiple users, use the below command	
Option 2	`msu(config)#access-list 2 permit 192.168.1.0 0.0.0.127`	Allows all users from the 1st network address of 192.168.1.0/25 (192.168.2-192.168.1.127)(NOTE: 192.168.1.127 is used instead of 192.168.1.126 because there is no actual subnetting occurs, the segmentation of the IP is used only for ranging the allowed users for the SSH access in the ACL rules
	`msu(config)#access-list 2 deny any`	Deny all other connections not permitted by the ACL
	`msu(config)#line vty 0 10`	Moves to vty line
	`msu(config)#access-class 2 in`	ACL is applied to all vty virtual interfaces in an inbound direction.

> **Note:**
> *When restricting access on vty lines, use access-class instead of access-group. Do not apply ACL intending to restrict traffic on a physical interface. If applied to physical interface, all packets are compared to the ACL before it can continue on its path to its destination. This can lead to a large reduction in the device performance. An ACL on a physical interface has to specify the SSH or Telnet port number that you are trying to deny. (Source: CCNA Routing and Switching Portable Command Guide, Scott Empson)*

specific interface. It is the basis of the switch if he thinks that the device is permitted to be connected to the network through that port or not. By default, switches discover the MAC address of a device when it is already physically connected. The MAC is registered dynamically into the CAM table.

Adding MAC address statically

Let us refer to the below topology

Figure 3-27 A switch with 2 PC

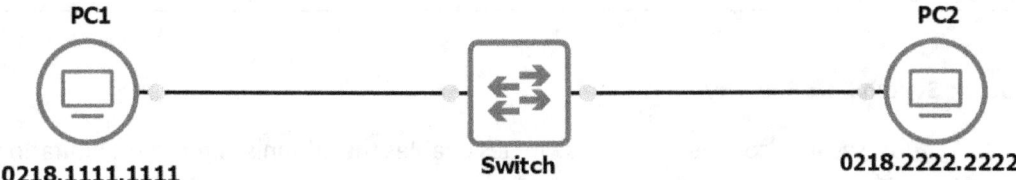

The topology here has 2 PCs connected to it. By default, their Physical addresses are added automatically to the CAM table with a type of **'dynamic'** once a network transaction occurs, such as sending of frame or packet. Refer to figure 3-28 for their address on the table

Figure 3-28 CAM table of the switch

```
Switch>en
Switch#show mac address-table
          Mac Address Table
-------------------------------------------

Vlan    Mac Address       Type        Ports
----    -----------       --------    -----

   1    0218.0222.0222    DYNAMIC     Fa0/2
   1    0218.1111.1111    DYNAMIC     Fa0/1
```

To set PC1's MAC address to static in the CAM table, use the following command:

| `switch(config)#`**`mac address-table static 0218.1111.1111 VLAN 1 int f0/1`** | Sets a permanent MAC address to interface f0/0 in VLAN 1 |

Figure 3-28 Update CAM table of the switch

```
Switch#show mac address-table
          Mac Address Table
-------------------------------------------

Vlan    Mac Address       Type        Ports
----    -----------       --------    -----

   1    0218.0222.0222    DYNAMIC     Fa0/2
   1    0218.1111.1111    STATIC      Fa0/1
```

Notice the figure 3-28; the type for MAC address 0218.1111.1111 has changed to static. To remove the statically added MAC Address, use the Following command.

Note: If the address type is changed, the entry is removed from the table until a network transaction occurs

`switch(config)#`**`no mac address-table static 0218.1111.1111 VLAN 1 int f0/1`**	Removes the statically added MAC address from the table

Static Switch Port Security

Port security configuration on switches enables the administrator to set limitations on the number of devices allowed to be connected on the switch. It also sets what will happen to the port if a violation has been discovered, especially when an unauthorized device connects to the network via switch. Below is a static approach to port security.

	`switch(config)#`**`int f0/1`**	Moves to interface configuration mode
	`switch(config)#`**`switchport mode access`**	Set the interface to access mode
	`switch(config)#`**`switchport port-security`**	Enable port-security on the interface
	`switch(config)#`**`switchport port-security max 2`**	Sets a maximum MAC address allowed in the interface.
	`switch(config)#`**`switchport port-security mac-address 0218.1111.1111`**	Sets a specific secure MAC address. Re-enter command to add another entry as prescribed on the max limit of port security
Setting Port Security Violation, Choose only one from the options below		
Option1	`switch(config)#`**`switchport port-security violation shutdown`**	The port is disabled when the switch does not recognize an unauthorized device whose MAC. A log entry is also created. When using shutdown, it may require a manual intervention to re-enable again the error disabled port.
Option2	`switch(config)#`**`switchport port-security violation restrict`**	Frames from an unauthorized address are dropped and a log entry is created. The interface remains operational.
Option 3	`switch(config)#`**`switchport port-security violation protection`**	Frames from an unauthorized address are dropped, but no log entry is created. The interface remains operational.

Dynamic Switch Port Security using Sticky MAC Addresses

Sticky MAC addresses set limitations to a switch port access to a specific MAC address that is learned dynamically. The addresses entered in this configuration are stored in the running configuration file. If saved, these MAC does not need to be relearned by the switch, and it provides a high level of switch port security.

Replace the static MAC using this command to enable sticky MAC	
`switch(config)#switchport port-security mac-address sticky`	All dynamically learned MAC are converted to sticky secure MAC addresses.

Interface ranging

Interface ranging is used especially when multiple ports have the same configuration. Instead of declaring a Single interface, use the below command to select all interface range declared

`switch(config)#int range f0/1-5`	Moves to interface configuration mode selecting five interfaces from f0/1 to f0/5

Verifying Switch Port Security

`switch#show port-security`	Displays security information for all interfaces
`switch#show port-security int f0/1`	Displays security information for interface f0/1
`switch#show port-security address`	Displays all secure MAC addresses configured on all switch interfaces
`switch#clear mac address-table dynamic`	Deletes all dynamically learned MAC Addresses
`switch#clear mac address-table dynamic address 0218.1111.1111`	Deletes the specified dynamic MAC Address
`switch#clear mac address-table dynamic int f0/1`	Deletes all dynamic MAC addresses on interface f0/1
`switch#clear mac address-table dynamic VLAN [VLAN_id]`	Deletes all dynamic MAC address on a specific VLAN id
`switch#clear mac address-table notification`	Clears MAC notification global counters

Recovering Automatically from Error-Disabled Port

Use the following commands to re-enable ports that were disabled due to violation shutdown

`switch(config)#errdisable recovery cause psecure-violation`	Enables the timer to recover from a port security violation disable state
`switch(config)#errdisable recovery interval [seconds]`	Specifies the time to recover from the err-disable state. The range is 30

	to 84,600 seconds. The default is 300 seconds.

> **Note:**
>
> *Disconnect the offending device first, otherwise, the port remains disabled, and the violation counter is incremented*
> *(Source: CCNA Routing and Switching Portable Command Guide, Scott Empson)*

Verifying Auto-recovery of Error-Disabled Ports

Command	Description
`switch#`**`show errdisable recovery`**	Displays error-disabled recovery timer information associated with each possible reason the switch could error-disable a port
`switch#`**`show interfaces status err-disabled`**	Displays Interface status or list of interface in error-disabled state
`switch#`**`clear errdisable interface`** `[interface_id VLAN (VLAN-list)]`	Re-enables all or specified VLANs that were error-disabled on an interface.

Loop Avoidance

CHAPTER 4

Spanning-tree Protocol

In the previous chapter, we discussed that providing redundant links, offers various issues and problems that may affect the network's performance. Manually shutting down the port of the redundant link may help solve the issue, but the problem is that it requires human intervention, especially when the active port cuts off. The network administrator needs to re-activate the disabled redundant link, which adds up to additional downtime.

In LAN switching, different standards were created to minimize the burden of the administrator in handling loops. In this chapter, we will present these well-known standards, the concepts that they perform, and how to execute them in the switching environment.

The Spanning-tree Protocol (STP) was originally created and introduced by the Digital Equipment Corporation (DEC), now Compaq. STP is a Layer 2 protocol that runs on Bridges and Switches. The specification of STP is IEEE 802.1D which is the standard used not just by cisco switches, also by other vendors. But later on, Cisco created their STP standard, the PVST+ where each VLAN has its own spanning-tree instance. The main purpose or task of STP is to make sure that no loop occurs in your network when you have redundant links.

STP Operations

How STP works? The way it does is it finds all links with redundancy, chooses that specific link, and shuts it down. How does the switch choose a link? This is done among switches in the network by electing a root bridge that will make decisions. This is similar to a Political Election campaign where voters have to choose their leader. Remember that there can only be one root bridge in a given network.

Root Bridge Election

How is the election process being done? Switches or bridges in a network running STP exchange information with a special Spanning-tree frame called *Bridge Protocol Data Unit (BPDU) Frames*. BPDUs send configuration messages at a regular interval using multicast frames. It contains the Bridge ID of each switch in the network exchanging their respective BPDUs to one another. The BPDU being sent by a switch is compared to the BPDU on the receiving switch. Parameters within the BPDU are examined and compared. The lesser it contains, the more it is elected.

The Bridge ID is the basis to determine the winner. A bridge ID is 8 bytes long which includes the Priority and MAC address of the switch. All Cisco switches running IEEE 802.1D have a default priority of 32,768.

> **Note:**
>
> To determine the root bridge, the priorities and MAC address are combined. If two switches or bridges have the same priority, then the MAC address is used to determine which one has the lowest ID.
>
> (Source: *Cisco Certified Network Associate Study Guide, Todd Lamle*).

Figure 4-1 Bridge ID

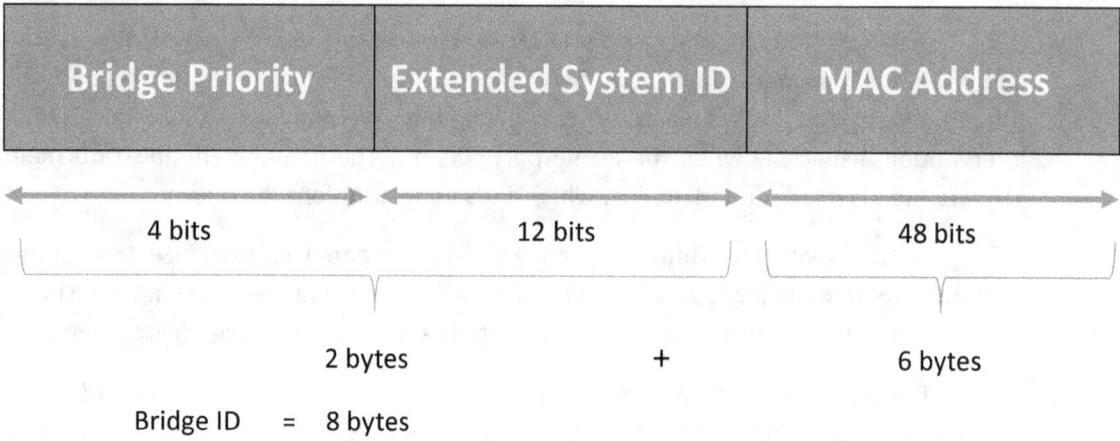

Now let us consider the below figure as an example for Root bridge election

Figure 4-2 Root Bridge election when priority is in default value

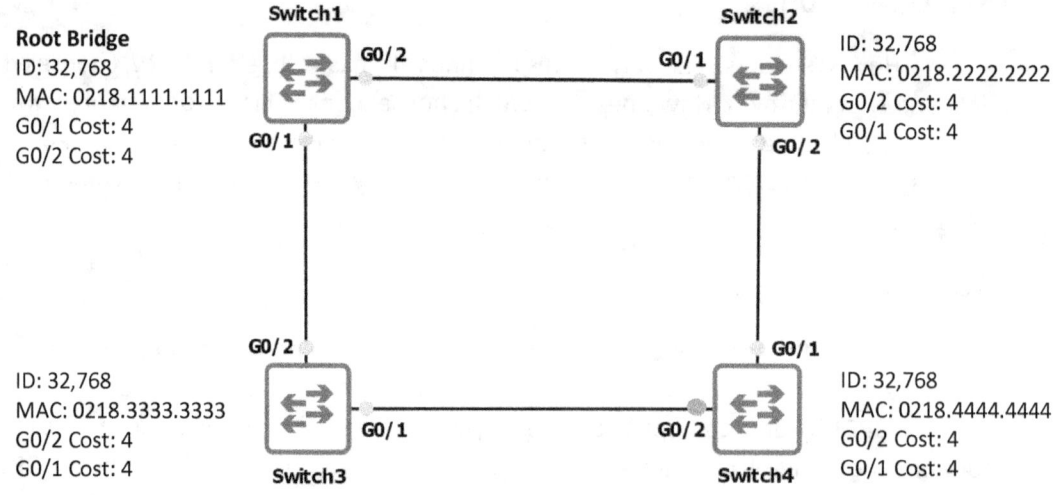

As you can see in Figures 4-2, all switches have default priority values. Since the priority is the same, the basis for the election is moved to the MAC Address. The rule is still the same; the device with the lowest MAC address will be the elected root bridge. In this case, Switch1 wins the election. So, what will happen now since Switch1 is the root bridge? He will now select what port to disable to stop the network loop.

Based on the above topology, Switch1 will disable port G0/2 at Switch4 because this switch has the highest Bridge ID of all the switches involved in the loop. Instead of Green color, the port will now be turned to Amber or Orange, indicating that it is now in the Blocking state. Now you might be wondering why G0/2 is not G0/1 at Switch4? To answer the question, refer to the following STP Sequence in case of a tie.

STP Sequence in case of a tie:

1. Lowest Root Bridge ID
2. Lowest Root Path Cost to Root Bridge
3. Lowest Sender Bridge ID
4. Lowest Sender Port ID

STP Port Roles

- **Root port** – One port on a switch that has the lowest cost to reach the root bridge and is it the forwarding state.
- **Designated Port** - selected on a per-segment (each link) basis, based on the cost to get back to root bridge for either side of the link. Designated ports are in the state of forwarding.
- **Alternate Port** – backup port for the designated port when the other side is not a root port. It is in the Blocking state

Port States

There are four common port states that switches or bridges running STP can transition through:

- **Disabled** – Spanning-tree is not enabled
- **Blocking** – It won't forward frames; listens to BPDUs. All orts are in a blocking state by default when the switched is powered on.
- **Listening** – Listens to BPDUs to make sure no loop occurs on the network before passing data frames.
- **Learning** – Learns MAC Addresses and builds a filter table but does not forward frames.
- **Forwarding** – Sends and receives all data on the bridge port.

Convergence occurs when bridges and switches transition to either the forwarding or blocking state. During this time, no data is forwarded. What it does is make sure that all devices have the same database. All data must be updated before data can be forwarded, but in convergence, updating takes time and usually takes 50 seconds to go from blocking to forwarding state.

Houtan Haddadlarijani stated in a cisco forum that STP transitioning time depends on what STP features you enabled. An STP-enabled port normally takes 20 seconds max aging time, then 15 seconds from listening to learning, and another 15 seconds from learning to forwarding.

That is why convergence takes up to 50 seconds. Using other features such as PortFast or BackboneFast improves the transition time, for it will skip other states leading it directly to the forwarding state. To sum up, it would take **30 to 50 seconds** after the switch is ready to forward any frames.

Now, let us go back to the previous topology we had. We will mark all ports with its corresponding roles.

Figure 4-3 Switched network with STP enabled.

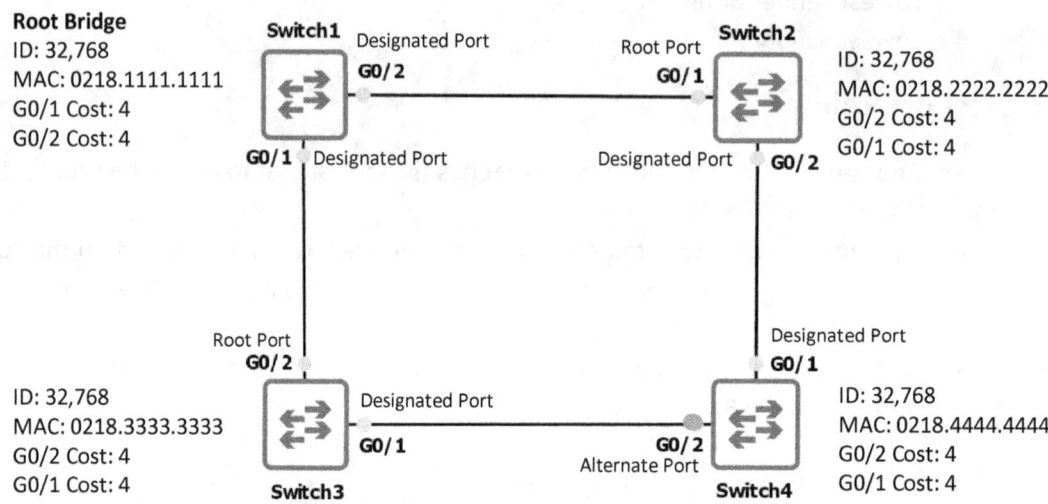

To check port roles, state and the Bridge ID of a switch in the Cisco CLI, use the following command:

| Switch1#**show spa** | Displays STP information |

The following are the display if you command show spa in the CLI

```
Switch 1
Switch1#show spa
VLAN0001
  Spanning tree enabled protocol ieee
  Root ID    Priority    32769
             Address     0218.1111.1111
             This bridge is the root
             Hello Time  2 sec Max Age 20 sec Forward Delay 15 sec

  Bridge ID  Priority    32769 (priority 32768 sys-id-ext 1)
             Address     0218.1111.1111
             Hello Time  2 sec Max Age 20 sec Forward Delay 15 sec
             Aging Time  20

Interface        Role Sts  Cost      Prio.Nbr  Type
---------------- ---- ---  --------- --------  ------------------------
```

```
    Gi0/1          Desg   FWD   4         128.25         P2p
    Gi0/2          Desg   FWD   4         128.26         P2p
```

Another way of identifying your device as the root bridge after the election has been completed is by checking the information displayed in the 'show spa.' You can easily determine if this switch is the root bridge by scanning through the result. Notice the result for switch1; every show spa result contains two Bridge ID information. The first one refers to the information about the root bridge, and the second refers to the current bridge or switch information. In this case, Switch1 is really the root bridge.

```
Switch 2
Switch1#show spa
VLAN0001
  Spanning tree enabled protocol ieee
  Root ID      Priority      32769
               Address       0218.1111.1111
               Cost          4
               Port          25(GigabitEthernet0/1)
               Hello Time    2 sec Max Age 20 sec Forward Delay 15 sec

  Bridge ID    Priority      32769 (priority 32768 sys-id-ext 1)
               Address       0218.2222.2222
               Hello Time    2 sec Max Age 20 sec Forward Delay 15 sec
               Aging Time    20

Interface           Role Sts   Cost       Prio.Nbr    Type
----------------    ---- ---   ---------  --------    --------------------
Gi0/1               Root FWD   4          128.25      P2p
Gi0/2               Desg FWD   4          128.26      P2p
```

```
Switch 3
Switch1#show spa
VLAN0001
  Spanning tree enabled protocol ieee
  Root ID      Priority      32769
               Address       0218.1111.1111
               Cost          4
               Port          26(GigabitEthernet0/2)
               Hello Time    2 sec Max Age 20 sec Forward Delay 15 sec

  Bridge ID    Priority      32769 (priority 32768 sys-id-ext 1)
               Address       0218.3333.3333
               Hello Time    2 sec Max Age 20 sec Forward Delay 15 sec
               Aging Time    20

Interface           Role Sts   Cost       Prio.Nbr    Type
----------------    ---- ---   ---------  --------    --------------------
Gi0/1               Desg FWD   4          128.25      P2p
Gi0/2               Root FWD   4          128.26      P2p
```

```
Switch 4
Switch1#show spa
VLAN0001
  Spanning tree enabled protocol ieee
  Root ID    Priority    32769
             Address     0218.1111.1111
             Cost        4
             Port        25(GigabitEthernet0/1)
             Hello Time  2 sec Max Age 20 sec Forward Delay 15 sec

  Bridge ID  Priority    32769 (priority 32768 sys-id-ext 1)
             Address     0218.4444.4444
             Hello Time  2 sec Max Age 20 sec Forward Delay 15 sec
             Aging Time  20

Interface       Role Sts  Cost       Prio.Nbr   Type
--------------- ---- ---  ---------  --------   --------------------------
Gi0/1           Root FWD  4          128.25     P2p
Gi0/2           Altn BLK  4          128.26     P2p
```

Path Cost

If you have notice the topology and the result of the show spa, you can see that there is a cost value equal to 4. What does this value stand for? Root path cost is used to determine the role of the port and whether or not traffic is blocked. It is also one of the determinants in the STP election sequence of ports when a tie exists. With path cost, you can also easily identify the speed of a link.

Basing from our example, the link has 1Gbps speed; refer to the below table.

Figure 4-4 IEEE Path Cost

Speed	New IEEE Cost	Old IEEE Cost
10Gbps	2	1
1Gbps	4	1
100Mbps	19	10
10Mbps	100	100

Note:

Older version is for 1900 series of Cisco Switches, new is to handle higher-speed links switches.

Modifying Path Cost

As the Administrator of the network, you may want to change the cost of each link. To do this, refer to the following commands.

Switch1(config)#**int f0/1**	Moves to interface configuration mode
Switch1(config-if)#**spanning-tree cost 100000**	Changes path cost, applicable to access port.
Switch1(config-if)#**spanning-tree VLAN [VLAN_id] cost 100000**	Configures the VLAN cost for an interface

> **Note:**
>
> *If a loop occurs, STP uses the path cost when trying to determine which interface to place into the forwarding state. A higher path cost means a lower speed transmission. The range of the cost keyword is 1 through 200000000. The default is based on the media speed of the interface.*
> *(Source: CCNA Routing and Switching Portable Command Guide, Scott Empson)*

STP Configuration

By default, cisco switches run in STP mode. If you want to know the configuration of setting the switches into STP, below is the command.

Switch1>**en**	Moves to privilege mode
Switch1#**config t**	Moves to Global configuration mode
Switch(config)#**spanning-tree mode pvst**	Set switch to PVST+ mode

Enable STP in a VLAN interface

This is an optional command since all switches along with the created VLANs are automatically configured to STP.

Switch1>**en**	Moves to privilege mode
Switch1#**config t**	Moves to Global configuration mode
Switch(config)#**spanning-tree VLAN [VLAN_id]**	Set specific VLAN to STP mode only

Manual Election

By default, switches choose their leader according to the lowest Bridge ID. Since all switches have the same Priority value by default, the MAC address becomes the next basis. It is recommended in a network setup that the root bridge or root switch be the device nearest to the router. To modify or change the priority value, there is a need for human intervention for the election of the root bridge.

There are two ways to make it done; below are the commands used to change the priority of a switch.

Using Priority Number

ROOT BRIDGE	
`Switch1>`**`en`**	Moves to privilege mode
`Switch1#`**`config t`**	Moves to Global configuration mode
`Switch(config)#`**`spanning-tree VLAN 1 priority 0`**	Set the current switch VLAN 1 to 1st Priority (Root Bridge)

SECONDARY ROOT SWITCH	
`Switch1>`**`en`**	Moves to privilege mode
`Switch1#`**`config t`**	Moves to Global configuration mode
`Switch(config)#`**`spanning-tree VLAN 1 priority 4096`**	Set the current switch VLAN 1 to 2nd Priority (Secondary Bridge)

Note:

If there is a third switch or more, to set the priority value, the increment value for the next switch is 4096 Also, if you have created multiple Vlans in the network, you must also set their priority same with vlan 1, this is to prevent loop.

Using Words

ROOT BRIDGE	
`Switch1>`**`en`**	Moves to privilege mode
`Switch1#`**`config t`**	Moves to Global configuration mode
`Switch(config)#`**`spanning-tree VLAN 1 root primary`**	Set the current switch VLAN 1 to primary

ROOT BRIDGE	
`Switch1>`**`en`**	Moves to privilege mode
`Switch1#`**`config t`**	Moves to Global configuration mode
`Switch(config)#`**`spanning-tree VLAN 1 root secondary`**	Set the current switch VLAN 1 to secondary root switch

Bridge Protocol Data Unit

BPDUs are hello packets sent out as multicast messages at definable intervals to exchange information among switches in the network. When the switch receives it, the switch uses a mathematical formula known as the Spanning-tree Algorithm (STA) to identify a switching loop in the network and determine which port needs to be disabled. It contains information regarding the Bridge ID, originating port, MAC Address, switch port priority, switchport cost, etc.

According to Omnisecu.com, two important BPDU frames switches exchange. The Configuration Bridge Protocol Data Unit (CBPDU) and the Topology Change Bridge Protocol Data Unit (TCBPDU). The CBPDU are sent between bridges to establish a network topology commonly generated from the Root Bridge. At the same time, TCBPDU is generated by non-root bridge switches and are sent after a topology change has been detected to indicate that the Spanning-tree Protocol algorithm should be initiated.

BPDU Frame Format

How does a switch understand other switches within the network? Switches always look up the ethernet frame scanning at the BDPU bytes. Only BPDU information is examined when the switches notice that a redundant link and switching loop exist. Below is the full-frame format broken down up to the BPDU contents.

Figure 4-5 802.3 Ethernet Frame Structure

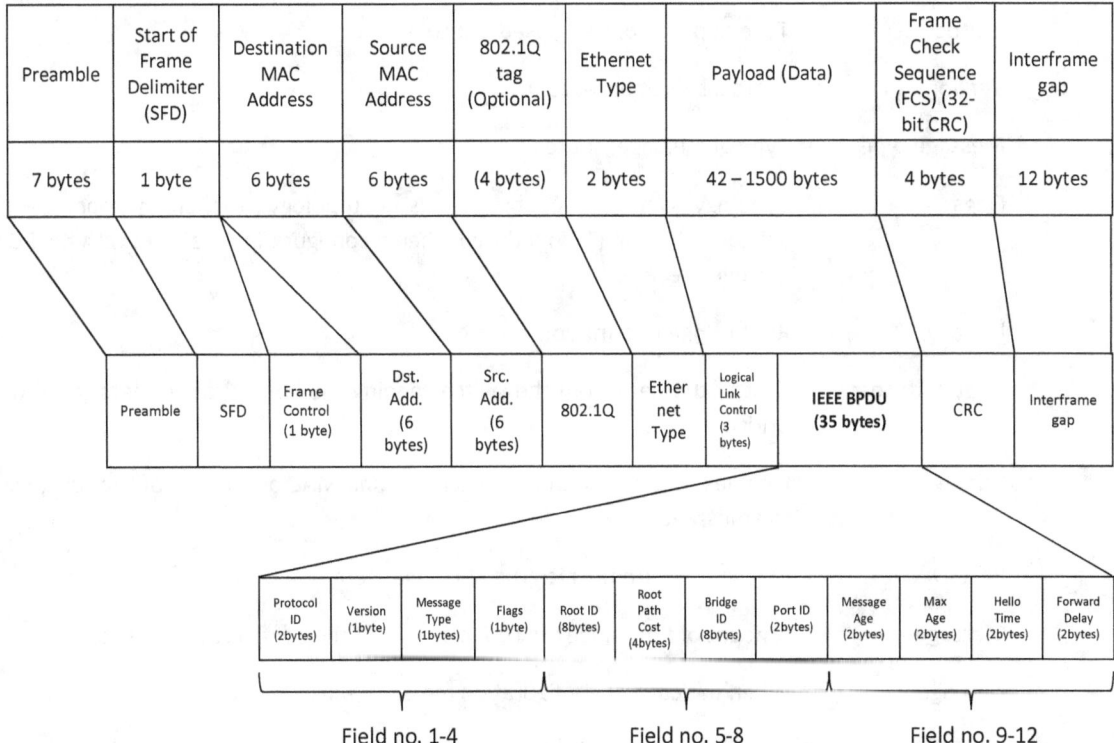

Figure 4-5 shows the structure of the frame up to the components of the BPDU. BDPU is a 32-byte header in a frame with several components on it. Each of which has specific roles in the hello frame. Below are the descriptions for each element.

Figure 4-6 Sample captured frame using Wireshark

(courtesy of netacad.com)

```
⊞ Frame 1 (60 bytes on wire, 60 bytes captured)
⊟ IEEE 802.3 Ethernet
  ⊞ Destination: Spanning-tree-(for-bridges)_00 (01:80:c2:00:00:00)
  ⊞ Source: Cisco_9e:93:03 (00:19:aa:9e:93:03)
    Length: 38
    Trailer: 0000000000000000
⊞ Logical-Link Control
⊟ Spanning Tree Protocol
    Protocol Identifier: Spanning Tree Protocol (0x0000)
    Protocol Version Identifier: Spanning Tree (0)
    BPDU Type: Configuration (0x00)
  ⊞ BPDU flags: 0x01 (Topology Change)
    Root Identifier: 24577 / 00:19:aa:9e:93:00
    Root Path Cost: 0
    Bridge Identifier: 24577 / 00:19:aa:9e:93:00
    Port Identifier: 0x8003
    Message Age: 0
    Max Age: 20
    Hello Time: 2
    Forward Delay: 15
```

Figure 4-7 BPDU format

Field	Description
Protocol ID	Type of protocol being used; set to 0
Version	Protocol version; set to 0
Message type	Type of message; set to 0
Flags	Topology change (TC) bit signals a topology a change; topology change acknowledgment (TCA) bit used when a configuration message with the TC bit set has been received
Root ID	Root bridge information
Root path cost	Cost of the path from the switch sending the configuration message to the root bridge
Bridge ID	Includes priority, extended system ID, and MAC address ID of the bridge sending the message
Port ID	Port number from which the BPDU was sent
Message age	Amount of time since the root bridge sent the configuration message
Max age	When the current configuration message will be deleted
Hello time	Time between root bridge messages
Forward delay	Time the bridges should wait before going to a new state

(Source: CCNA6, Scaling Networks. www.netacad.com)

802.1D BPDU Propagation and Process

The following information explains the process and propagation of BPDU in a switched network:

1. By default, each switch in a network thinks and assumes that he is the root bridge until BPDU frames are sent, and the calculation of STP is executed.

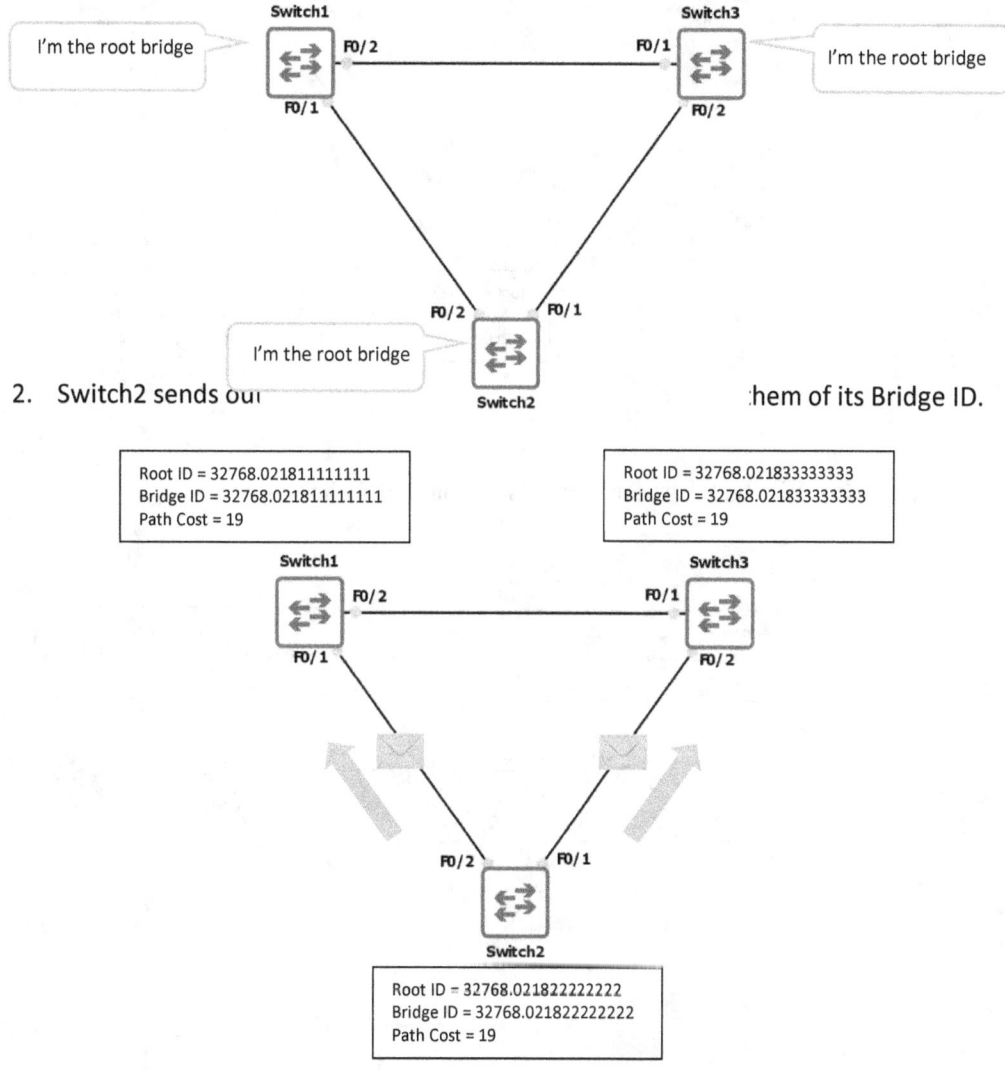

2. Switch2 sends out BPDU frames to inform them of its Bridge ID.

3. Switch1 and Switch3 will compare their respective Bridge IDs from the BPDU sent by Switch2 to determine the Root Bridge. Once received, they will update their Root ID to the lowest ID. Switch1 sees that his ID is lower than Switch2; therefore, he will ignore the frame from Switch2. While Switch3 sees that Switch2 has lower ID, Switch3 will update its root ID.

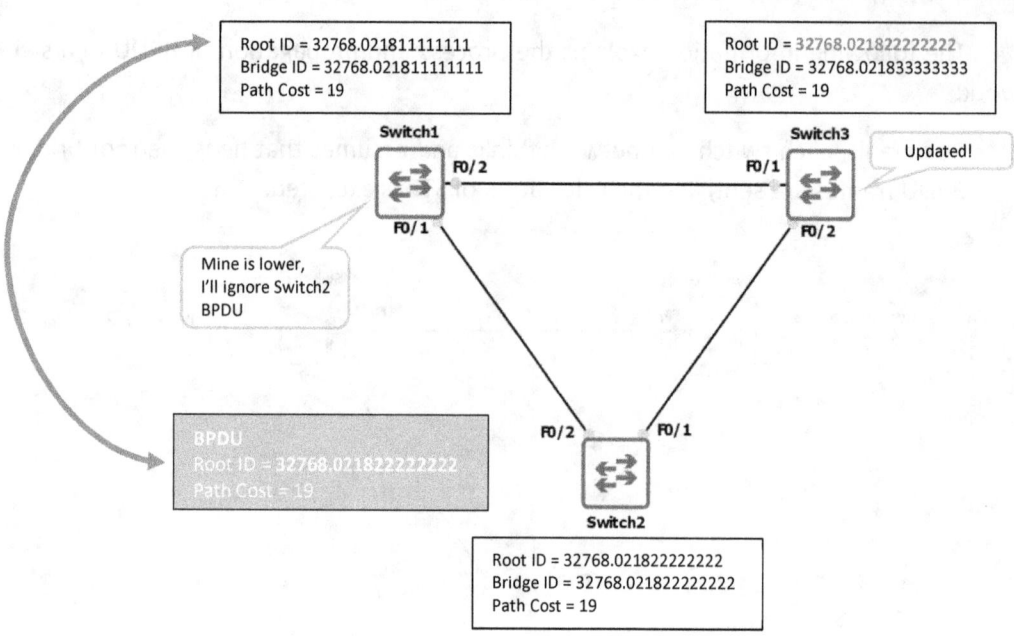

4. Switch3 sends BPDU out all ports saying that Switch2 is the root bridge.

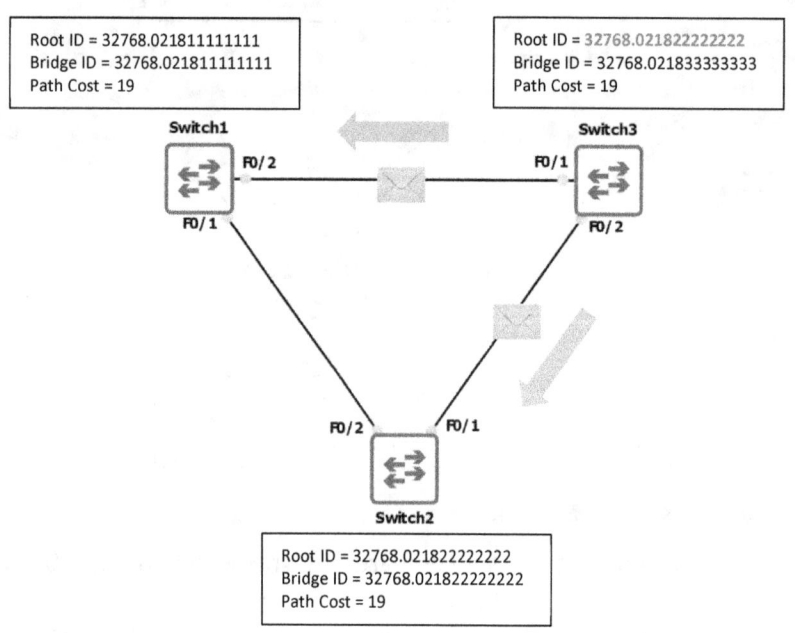

5. Switch2 will compare the information from Switch3, with the content of the message, Switch2 still thinks that he is the Root Bridge. While Switch1, since it still has the lowest ID, the BPDU again will be ignored.

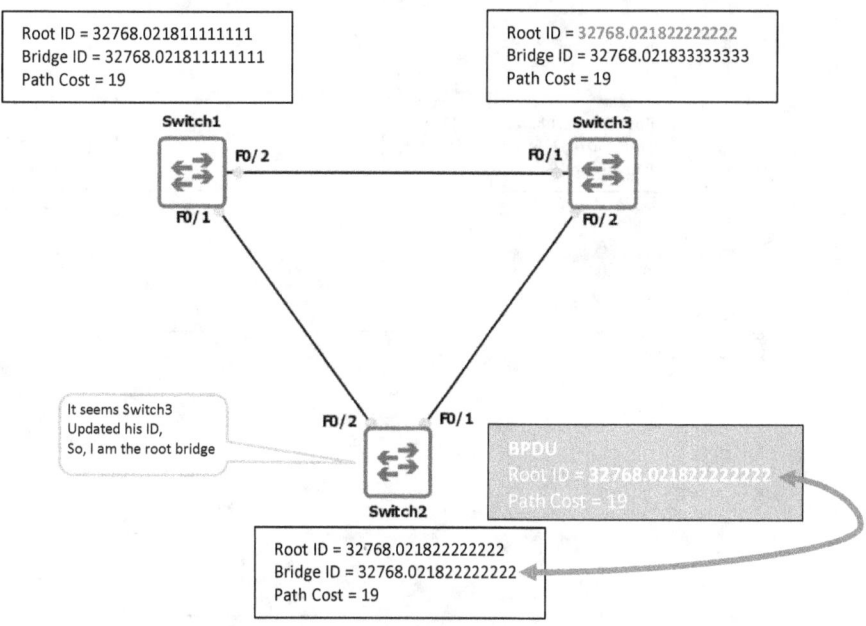

6. Switch1 will now send BPDU of its own that contains information designated Switch1 as the root bridge.

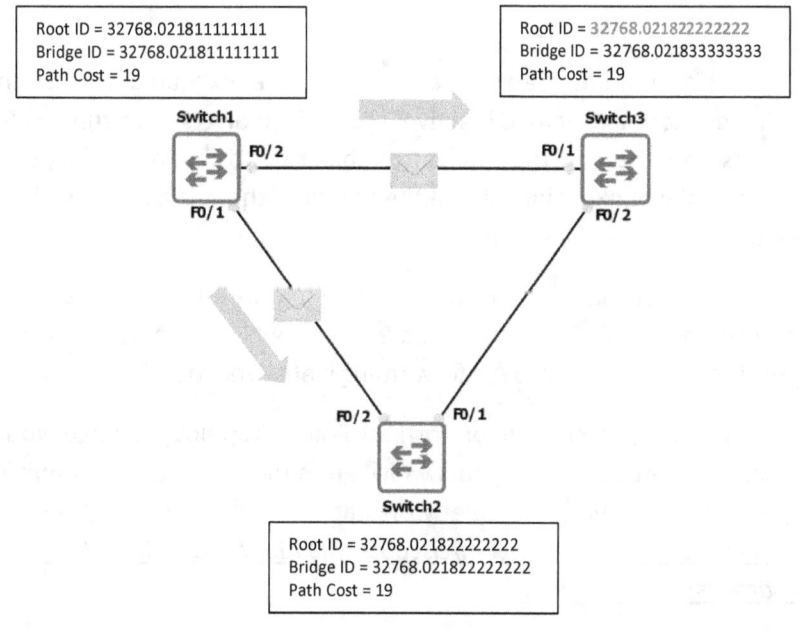

7. Switch3 and Switch2 compare the information received from Switch1 so, they have now realized that the stored root bridge information on their respective database is not correct. Both of them will update the information showing Switch1 as the root bridge.

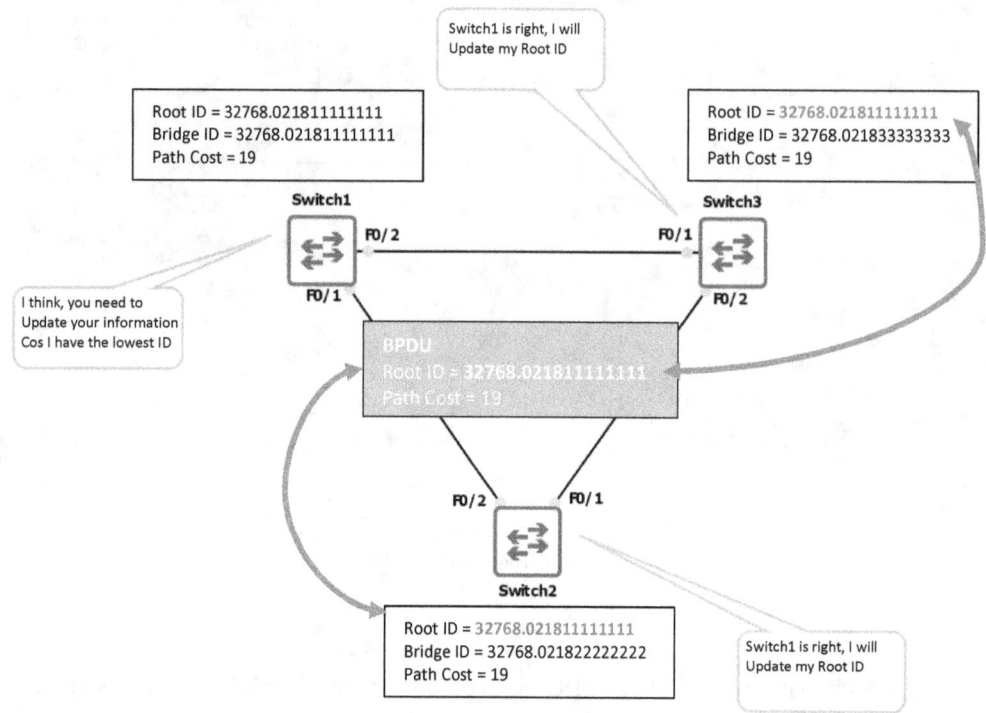

PortFast

PortFast is configured where loops are never expected because they connect end-users, not switches. Normally, if a PC is actively connected on a switch running STP, it would take up to 50 seconds until the port transitions from blocking to the forwarding state. With 50 seconds of downtime in the banking industry in the network, there is a big loss of income since there is no transaction under that 50 seconds.

Because of that, Cisco came up with a feature that would at least improve the period of port transitioning. This feature is called PortFast, which bypasses the listening and learning state and puts the port directly into the forwarding state, which lowers the convergence to 30 seconds.

Another Characteristic of PortFast is that Topology Change Notification (TCN) BPDU is never sent for port up/down events which gives the advantage of simplified TCN transmission in a large network when multiple workstations are coming up or shutting down. *(Source: https://www.certificationkits.com/cisco-certification/ccna-articles/cisco-ccna-switching/cisco-ccna-port-fast-a-bpdu-guard/)*

Figure 4-8 Where a PortFast should be enabled

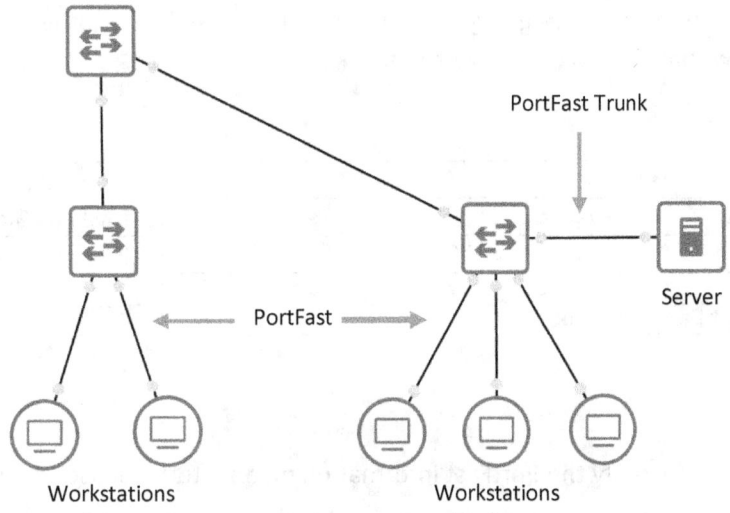

Note:
STP is never disabled on a port running PortFast. If ever BPDU is heard, the port losses the PortFast status. It is also recommended that do not enable PortFast on trunk links which connects a switch to another switch for it could cause bridging or switching loops and broadcast storms since the port never goes to Listening and Learning state. (Source: https://www.certificationkits.com/cisco-certification/ccna-articles/cisco-ccna-switching/cisco-ccna-port-fast-a-bpdu-guard/)

PortFast Configuration

Configuration of PortFast can be done either Globally or Per-interface basis. Let us think of a simple network with an interface f0/1 connected to a PC. Refer to the following commands.

Globally

`Switch>`**`en`**	Moves to privilege mode
`Switch#`**`config t`**	Moves to Global configuration mode
`Switch(config)#`**`spanning-tree portfast default`**	Enables Edge PortFast on all Switch Ports that are non-trunking.

Per-interface

`Switch>`**`en`**	Moves to privilege mode
`Switch#`**`config t`**	Moves to Global configuration mode
`Switch(config)#`**`int f0/1`**	Moves to interface configuration mode
`Switch(config-if)#`**`spanning-tree portfast`**	Enables Edge PortFast on an Access Port.

PortFast can also be configured on a trunk link provided that the trunk link is a server connection or a path going to a router and not a link to another layer 2 devices. Let us assume below that interface f0/1 is a trunk link going to a Server.

`Switch>`**`en`**	Moves to privilege mode
`Switch#`**`config t`**	Moves to Global configuration mode
`Switch(config)#`**`int f0/1`**	Moves to interface configuration mode
`Switch(config-if)#`**`spanning-tree portfast trunk`**	Enables PortFast on a Trunk Port

To verify the PortFast information on an interface, use the below command

`Switch#`**`show spanning-tree int f0/1 portfast`**	Shows the PortFast information on interface f0/1

BPDU Guard

We have learned that PortFast is configured commonly on links that are non-trunk which are connections from the switch going to a workstation or PC. But, what if you have accidentally or unintentionally configured a PortFast on a port that is going to another switch, for instance? A bridging loop will occur. Another is what if you are a service provider? Then a client of yours connects his switch to your network that is configured with PortFast? The next worst thing is the switch of your client has a lower Bridge ID than yours, so it would only mean that your client's switch will be elected as the new root bridge.

BPDU guard is created to protect the STP topology of your network from these problems by moving a non-trunking port into an 'errdisable' state when a BPDU is received on that port. If BPDU guard is enabled on the switch, when it hears a BPDU, the spanning-tree will shut down the port with PortFast enabled interfaces instead of moving them into a spanning tree blocking state.

Remember, in a valid setup, no BPDU is received on PortFast-configured Interfaces unless there is an invalid configuration because the administrator had to put back the interface in service manually.

Refer to the following figures in case BPDU guard is enabled or disabled.

Figure 4-9 With BPDU Guard Enabled

SP1 is Root Bridge

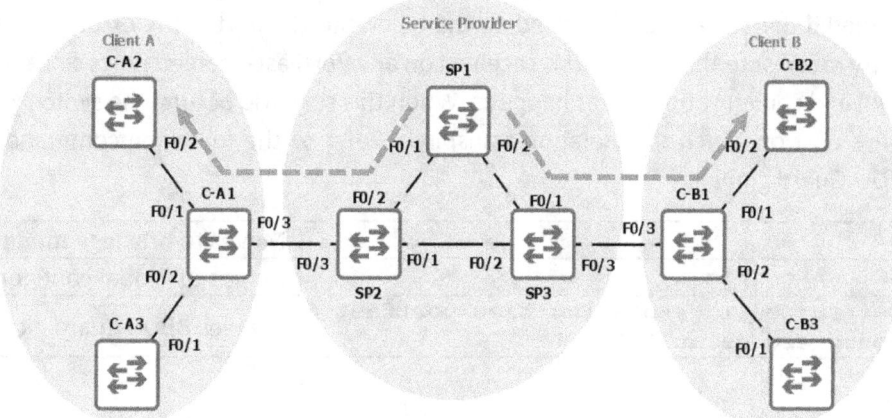

If enabled, the traffic flow will start from the root bridge in the Service Provider network regardless of the Bridge ID of the switches from clients A and B connected to the Provider.

While if disabled, the STP topology will be modified and will look for the Lowest Bridge ID within the entire network, including the two clients; from there, switches will choose and elect a new Root Bridge. In the below figure, let us assume that Switch C-B3 from client B has a lower Bridge ID; it will become the newly designated Root Bridge. Switches within the Service Provider will announce and inform all other switches that Switch C-B3 is the Root Bridge. Since there is a change in the topology, the traffic flow will be exactly what the figure below represents.

Figure 4-10 With BPDU Guard Disabled

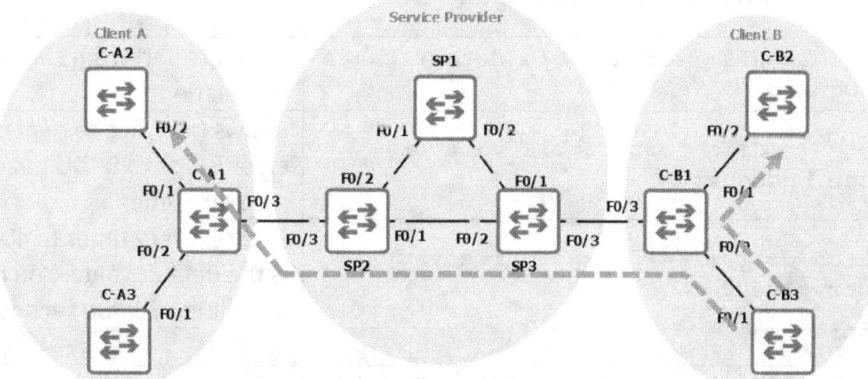

C-B3 is the New Root

BPDU Guard Configuration

BPDU guard can be configured either globally or per-interface but the feature works differently.

- **Globally**

In the global approach, Spanning-tree shuts down ports that are configured PortFast-enabled if there is a BPDU received on them and put the port in the error-disabled state. We are pretty much sure that no BPDU is received on any PortFast-enabled ports since it could only mean an invalid configuration if that happens. When this scenario occurs, the switch will shut down the entire port on which the violation transpires. Refer to the following commands in enabling the BPDU Guard globally

`Switch>`**`en`**	Moves to privilege mode
`Switch#`**`config t`**	Moves to Global configuration mode
`Switch(config)#`**`spanning-tree portfast bpduguard default`**	Enables BPDU guard globally

- **Per-Interface**

When the interface receives a BPDU, it moves the interface to an error-disabled state.

`Switch>`**`en`**	Moves to privilege mode
`Switch#`**`config t`**	Moves to Global configuration mode
`Switch(config)#`**`int range f0/1-5`**	Enters interface range configuration mode
`Switch(config-if-range)#`**`spanning-tree portfast bpduguard enable`**	Enables BPDU guard on all ports within the range

Use the below commands to prevent the port from shutting down. Other commands related to BPDU Guard are shown below.

`Switch(config)#`**`errdisable detect cause bpduguard`**	Prevents port from shutting down due to violation
`Switch(config)#`**`errdisable recovery cause bpduguard`**	Allows interface to re activate itself if error is due to BPDU guard by setting a recovery timer
`Switch(config)#`**`errdisable recovery interval 400`**	Sets recovery timer to 400 seconds. 300 is the default value. You can choose from 30 to 86,400 seconds.
Other Commands	
`Switch(config)#`**`spanning-tree bpduguard disable`**	Disables BPDU Guard
`Switch#`**`show spanning-tree summary totals`**	Checks if BPDU Guard is enabled or disabled
`Switch#`**`show errdisable recovery`**	Shows errdisable recovery timer information

BPDU Filtering

BPDU filtering helps you secure and avoid the transmission of BPDUs on ports where PortFast is enabled connected to an end system. It can be configured either globally or per interface.

Globally

`Switch>`**`en`**	Moves to privilege mode
`Switch#`**`config t`**	Moves to Global configuration mode
`Switch(config)#`**`spanning-tree portfast bpdufilter default`**	Enables BPDU filter globally

Per-Interface

`Switch>`**`en`**	Moves to privilege mode
`Switch#`**`config t`**	Moves to Global configuration mode
`Switch(config)#`**`int range f0/1-5`**	Enters the interface range configuration mode
`Switch(config-if-range)#`**`spanning-tree bpdufilter enable`**	Enables BPDU filter in the interfaces within the range

To disable BPDU filter, use the below command.

`Switch(config)#`**`no spanning-tree portfast bpdufilter default`**	Disables BPDU filter globally

UplinkFast

In a hierarchical network, switches can be grouped into the backbone, distribution, and access switches. The below figure shows a complex network where switches on the distribution and access layer have at least one redundant link that the spanning-tree blocks to prevent loops.

Figure 4-11 Switches in a Hierarchical Network

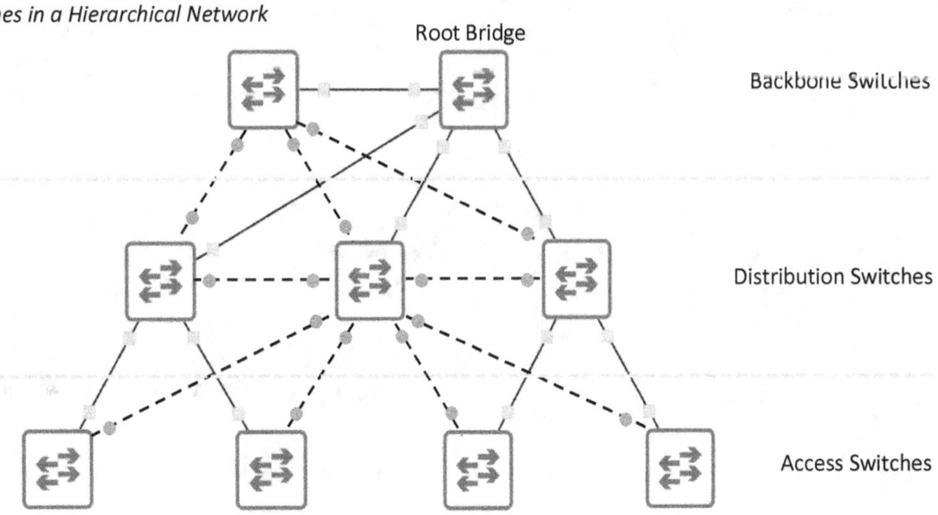

In this type of setup, if there is a failure in a switch's active link, it will use the alternate path as soon as the spanning tree selects a new root port. Using the UplinkFast will provide fast convergence using the uplink groups in the access layer after a change in the spanning-tree topology occurs. The UplinkFast will accelerate the choice of a new root port when a switch or a link fails, or the spanning tree reconfigures itself. Refer to the following figures as an example

Figure 4-12 Example of a network with UplinkFast Enabled before direct active link fails

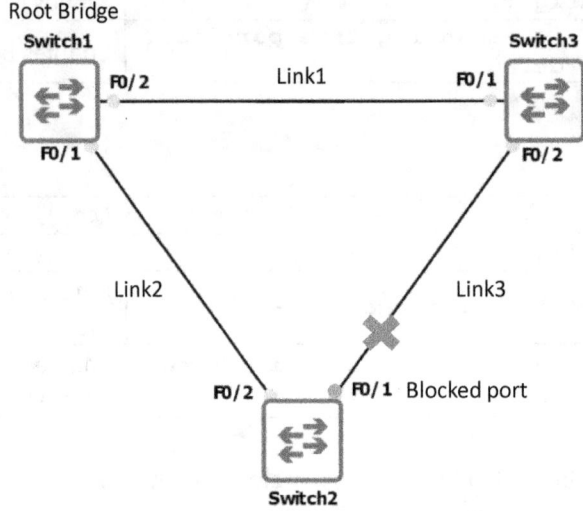

Figure 4-12 shows that Switch1, the root bridge, has a direct active link to switches 3 and 2. In this topology, Switch2 has the highest Bridge ID. Notice that Switch2 port f0/1 is moved to a blocking state because of STP since we assume that Switch2 has the highest bridge ID.

When Link2 of Switch2 goes to the root bridge fails, if UplinkFast is configured, it will unblock the port in the blocking state and transition it immediately to the forwarding state. It would take approximately 1 to 5 seconds for the switchover.

Figure 4-13 Example of a network with UplinkFast Enabled after direct active link fails

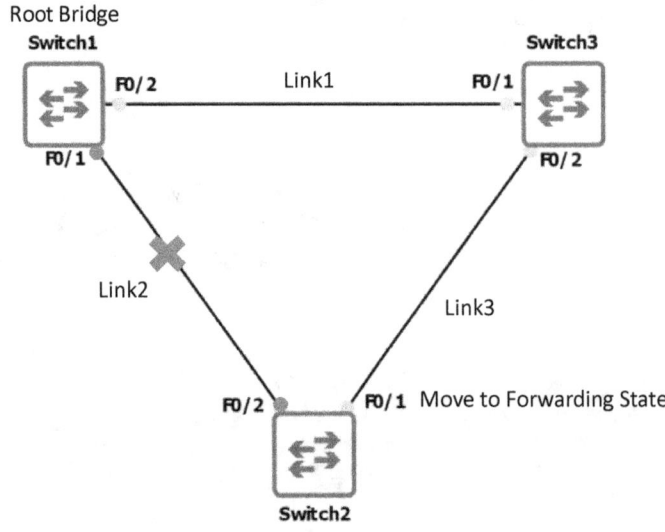

The moment the switch transitions the alternate link to forwarding state, the switch will start to flood dummy multicast frames on the concerned port, one for each entry in the Local Enhanced Address Recognition Logic (EARL) table except entries that are affiliated with the failed root port. By default, about 15 dummy multicast frames are sent per 100 ms.

Each dummy multicast frame will use its station address as its source MAC address from the EARL table with a dummy multicast address (01-00-0C-CD-CD-CD) as its destination MAC address.

When switches receive the dummy multicast frames, they instantly update their respective EARL table for each source MAC address to utilize the alternate port as the new port, allowing the switches almost immediately to use it as a new path.

Suppose the link from the previously active root port is restored. In that case, switches will have to wait for a period that is doubled the forward delay time and another 5 seconds before fully re-activating the port to the forwarding state. This process helps the neighboring port to have more time to converge through the listening and learning states to the forwarding state.

UplinkFast Configuration

VLANs with switch priority have been modified are not possible for enabling UplinkFast. To configure UplinkFast, the switch priority should be set to default first because if configured, UplinkFast affects all VLANs on the switch; it is not per VLAN basis.

If your switch is running RSTP and MSTP mode, you can still configure UplinkFast, but the feature will be disabled or inactive until the mode is set again to PVST+

Below is how you configure UplinkFast.

`Switch>`**`en`**	Moves to privilege mode
`Switch#`**`config t`**	Moves to Global configuration mode
`Switch(config)#`**`spanning-tree UplinkFast [max-update rate`** *pkts-per-seconds***`]`**	Enables UplinkFast. (Optional) For pkts-per-second, the default is 150, but you can choose from range 0 to 32000. If the rate is set to 0, station-learning frames are not generated, and the spanning-tree topology transitions more slowly after a link failure.

> **Note:**
> *UplinkFast is most useful in wiring-closet switches that have a limited number of active VLANs. This enhancement might not be useful for other types of applications and should not be enabled on backbone or distribution layer switches.*
> *(Source:https://www.cisco.com/c/en/us/td/docs/switches/lan/catalyst4000/82glx/configuration/guide/stp_enha.html)*

BackboneFast

The BackboneFast is somehow similar to UplinkFast; the only difference is that it provides fast convergence at the backbone level of the network when a change of Spanning-tree topology occurs.

It detects link breaks or link failure on paths that are not directly connected to the switch, which happens when the switch receives inferior BPDU from its designated bridge on its root port or blocked ports.

The inferior BPDU is a signal that tells the switch that the designated bridge might have lost its connection to the root bridge, and BackboneFast will have to find an alternate path to the root. It also identifies a switch that declares itself as both the root and designated bridge.

Normally, in the spanning-tree rules specified in IEEE, the switch ignores inferior BPDUs for the configured maximum aging time. But, BackboneFast uses them because as soon as one inferior BPDU is received, it is sure that a failure has existed on the link going to the root and that at least one port should be aged out.

BackboneFast Operation

The switch will try to look for an alternative path going to the root bridge. When the inferior BPDU is received on the blocked port, all other ports, such as the root port and blocked interfaces on that switch, become an alternate path to the root bridge.

If these BPDUs are received on the root port, all blocked interfaces are transformed into alternate paths to the bridge. If ever these BPDUs are received on the root port. At the same time, there are no blocked ports; the switch will assume that it has lost its connectivity to the root bridge, which causes the maximum aging time on the root port to expire and becomes the root bridge according to normal spanning-tree rules.

If a switch has alternate paths destined to the root bridge, it will use these alternate paths to send a new type of protocol data unit (PDU) known as the Root Link Query (RLQ) PDU, which is a request transmitted out all alternate paths to the root bridge, and it will wait for an RLQ response from other switches in the network

If the switch finds out that an alternate path still exists to the root, it expires the maximum aging time on the port that received the inferior BPDU.

Suppose two or more alternate path is still able to connect. In that case, the switch will transform all ports on which it received an inferior BPDU as its designated ports and transition them from the blocking state through the listening and learning into the forwarding state.

Refer to the following figures that explain how BackboneFast works in the network.

Figure 4-14 Example of a network with BackboneFast Enabled before not directly-connected link fails

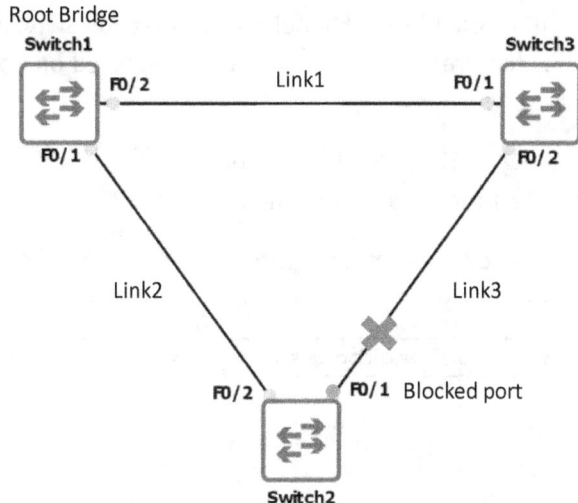

Figure 4-14 shows a sample network where Switch1 is the root bridge and is connected to Switch3 over link1 and Switch 2 over link2. The direct link from Switch2 going to Switch3 is blocking.

Let us say that link1 has failed, so Switch2 will detect the failure as an indirect failure since link1 is not a direct link for Switch2. Since the link has failed, the Switch3 has no longer available path to the root bridge for link3 is currently blocking. So, this is where the BackboneFast takes place. The BackboneFast will allow the blocked port on Switch2 to transition immediately to listening state and not wait for the port's maximum aging time to expire. The BackboneFast will transition the blocked port to the forwarding state, which will pave the way for Switch3 to Switch1. It would take 30 seconds for the switchover. Refer to the below figure.

Figure 4-15 Example of a network with BackboneFast Enabled after not directly-connected link fails

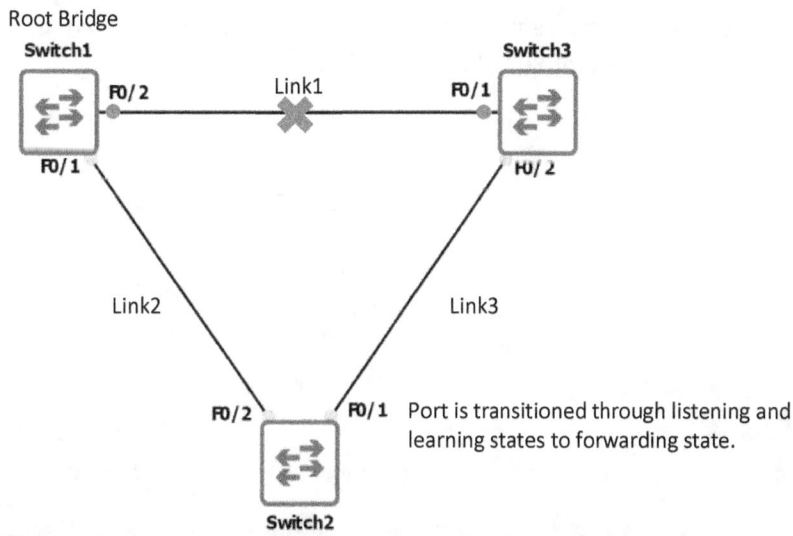

Note:
If a new switch is introduced into a shared-medium topology, BackboneFast is not activated. The new switch begins sending inferior BPDUs, which indicate that it is the root switch. However, the other switches ignore these inferior BPDUs and the new switch learns that Switch B is the designated bridge to Switch A, the root switch. (Source:https://www.cisco.com/c/en/us/td/docs/switches/lan/catalyst4000/8-2glx/configuration/guide/stp_enha.html)

BackboneFast Configuration

If you want to enable BackboneFast, all of your switches in the network should be configured with this feature. Remember, it is not supported on Token Ring VLANS, but it can be used with third-party switches.

When running RSTP or MSTP, BackboneFast can still be configured, but the feature remains disabled unless the mode is switched back to PVST+.

Refer to the following command for BackboneFast configuration.

`Switch>`**`en`**	Moves to privilege mode
`Switch#`**`spanning-tree backbonefast`**	Enables BackboneFast

Rapid Spanning-tree Protocol

Let us recall the time for the ports to transition to the forwarding state using the IEEE 802.1D standard, also known as STP. In cisco, we have used the standard of PVST+ that is a per-VLAN basis on behalf of STP. The STP, a protocol that helps the network administrator prevent the occurrence of switching loops, has helped the network perform well. With the advent of some newly created or innovated technology that requires a faster process, to cope up, a new feature that replaces STP was designed since STP is somehow not anymore suitable to be used in these type of network requirement that requires rapid process since the STP takes for about a minute for the ports to work.

The Rapid Spanning-tree Protocol with an IEEE standard of 802.1W, was designed to address the network need for faster convergence of ports. Though PortFast, UplinkFast, and BackboneFast are there to speed up the convergence time of a bridged network, these features are limited to Cisco devices only since they are proprietary of Cisco. RSTP is an evolution of the 802.1D since the concept is just the same but is more improved. In cisco, we use Rapid PVST+ as the representation of 802.1W.

RSTP Port States

Compared to STP, which has five port states, the RSTP is simplified into three operational states. The ***discarding, learning, and forwarding***. The RSTP merged the blocking and listening state of the STP into one unique 802.1W discarding state.

Figure 4-16 RSTP Port States

STP (802.1D)	RSTP (802.1W)	Port included in active topology	Port learns MAC Addresses
Disable	Discarding	No	No
Blocking	Discarding	No	No
Listening	Discarding	Yes	No
	Learning	Yes	Yes
	Forwarding	Yes	Yes

RSTP Port Roles

There are four common port roles in RSTP mode, namely:

- **Root port** – It is the port that receives the best BPDU on a bridge. It is the port closest to the root bridge, ports that are in the direction going to the root bridge.
- **Designated Port** – A port that can send the best BPDU on the segment it is connected to.
- **Alternate Port** – a port that receives useful BPDU from another switch and is blocking. Provides an alternate path to the root bridge.
- **Backup Port** – a port that receives useful BPDU from the same switch and is blocking. A backup port or link to other switches that provided redundancy to the same segment does not guarantee an alternate link going to the root bridge.

Figure 4-17 RSTP Port Roles

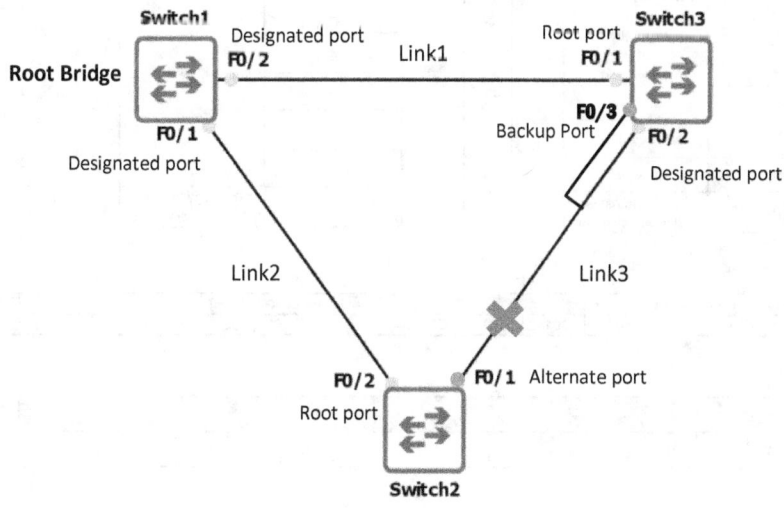

New BPDU Format

Another unique thing with RSTP is that it introduces a new BPDU format. The BPDU for RSTP is of type 2 or version 2, wherein legacy bridges are easy to detect since it drops this new type of BPDU. Next, instead of using just 2 bits (STP flag), the RSTP uses all 8 bits of the Flag byte that performs the following:

- Encode the port roles and states where the BPDU came from
- Proposal/Agreement mechanism handling

Figure 4-18 IEEE 802.3/802.2 LLC frame: 802.1D BPDU vs 802.1W BPDU

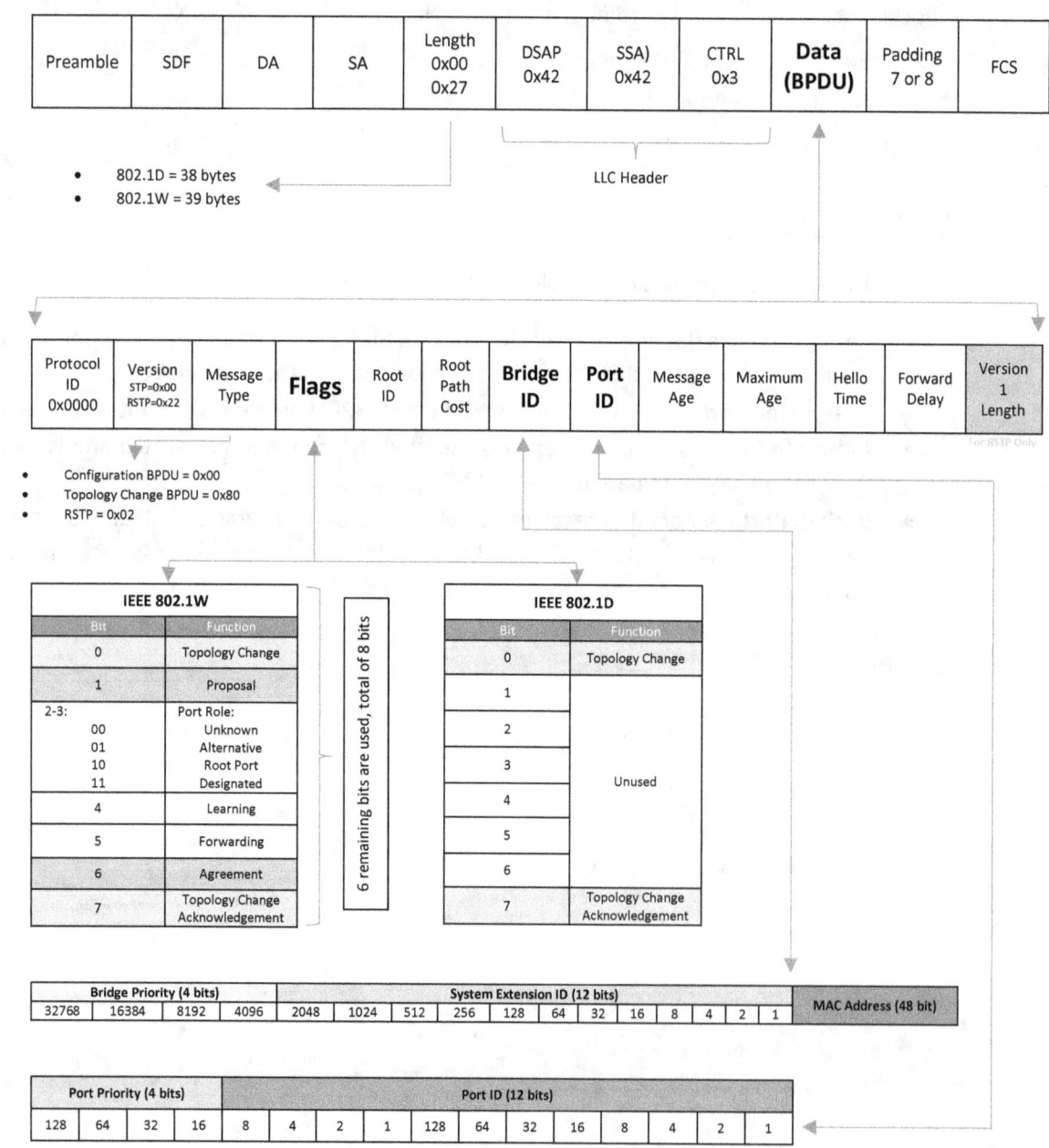

RSTP BPDU management

Let us recall in the 802.1D that BPDUs are relayed more than generated, and a non-root bridge generates BPDUs only if it receives another BDPU on the root port. In RSTP, a BPDU is sent holding its current information every given hello-time second even no BPDU is received from the root port.

If a BPDU is not received within three consecutive times on a port, its information can immediately age out. Due to some changes in that information, BPDUs became a *keep-alive mechanism* between bridges or switches. A particular switch may consider that it loses its connectivity to the root or designated bridge once these three (3) consecutive BPDUs are missed. This aging process promotes rapid failure detection wherein once a bridge, or a switch fails to receive any BPDU from its neighbor, it only means that it loses its connection.

Another new thing with regards to the BPDU in the RSTP mode is it accepts Inferior BPDU *(recall inferior BPDU from STP BackboneFast),* which then paves the way for a switch that loses a direct link to the root bridge to divert its root port to another interface leading to another switch that has a direct connection to the root bridge.

Rapid Port Transitioning

802.1W can transition the port into a forwarding state safely, not relying on any timer configuration. New feedback mechanism is introduced in this mode for all switches that can run RSTP. To make the rapid convergence on a port possible, the 802.1W relies on the edge ports and link type

Edge Ports – This is similar to the PortFast feature, where all ports directly connected to the end stations cannot create switching or bridging loops in the network which means it is a link pointing to workstations only. Because of this, ports linked to end stations are immediately transitioned to the forwarding state. To configure edge port, it is recommended by Cisco to use the PortFast configuration.

Figure 4-19 Edge Ports

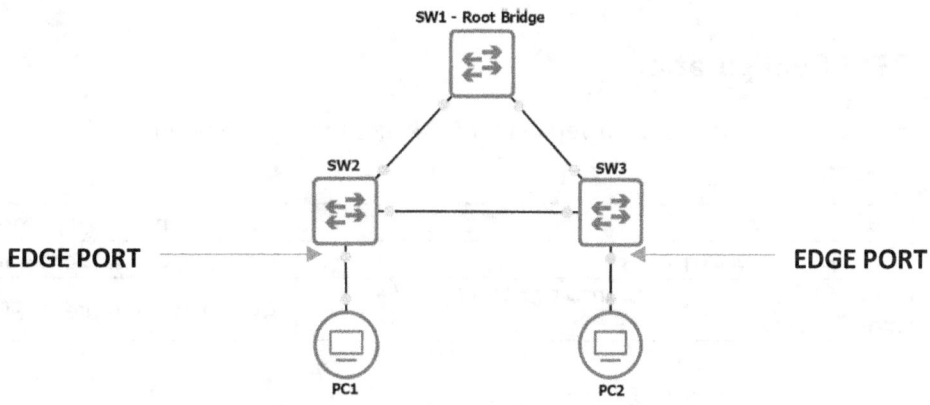

Link Type – Another basis for fast convergence of RSTP is the link type used in the network. Types of links can be identified by the following:

- Point-to-point refers to a point-to-point link between switches and a link from a switch going to an end station working in a full-duplex mode.
- Shared – a port working in half-duplex mode usually links from the Hub to a Switch or an end station.

Figure 4-20 Link Type

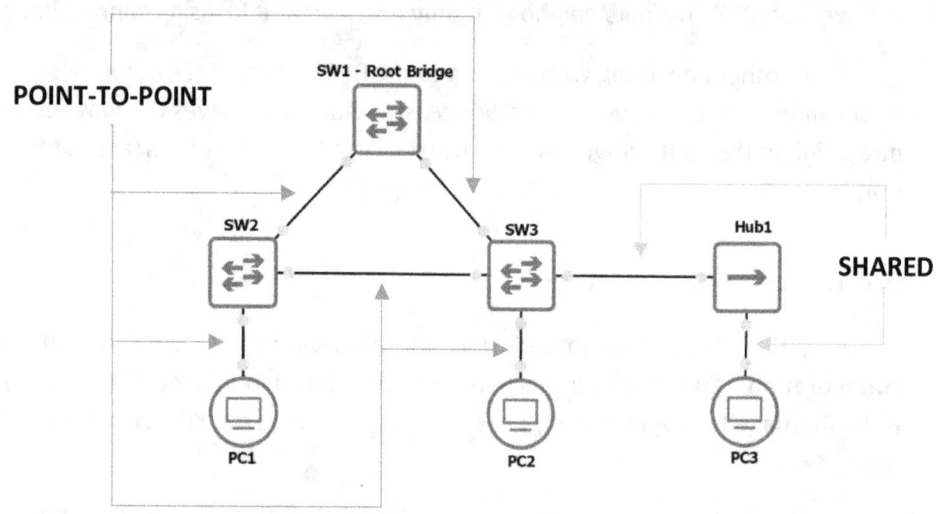

Rapid Convergence

The convergence in 802.1W is still the same with 802.1D; the only new thing with RSTP is that an acknowledgment takes place on the switch's new root port for the immediate transition of the port to the forwarding state and bypasses the twice-the-forward-delay long listening and learning states which lowers the convergence to a maximum time of 6 seconds.

RSTP Configuration

To enable the Cisco version for RSTP, use the below command.

`Switch1>`**`en`**	Moves to privilege mode
`Switch1#`**`config t`**	Moves to Global configuration mode
`Switch1(config)#`**`spanning-tree mode rapid-pvst`**	Set switch to Rapid PVST+ mode.

If you have a legacy switch running 802.1D connected to a switch with 802.1W, it is good to use the below command if you ever decide to replace the legacy switch to a newer device running RSTP or MSTP. The reason is that your current switch, which is running RSTP previously connected with a legacy switch, is expecting an 802.1D BPDU even if the legacy was changed to a newer device. That happens because of the so-called built-in protocol migration mechanism. To resolve the issue, it is good to conduct a renegotiation.

`Switch1>en`	Moves to privilege mode
`Switch1#config t`	Moves to Global configuration mode
`Switch1(config)#clear spanning-tree detected-protocols`	Conducts a renegotiation to neighboring switches restarting the protocol migration mechanism.

Multiple Spanning-tree Protocol

Recall from the previous STP types we have discussed that VLAN has its instances. For this portion, it comes a different approach. Defined in IEEE 802.1s standard is a protocol that allows multiple spanning trees or models for each VLAN onto a single physical network.

MSTP, as an extension to RSTP, reduces the spanning-tree instances needed in a bridged network that has multiple VLANs. It configures a distinct spanning-tree per VLAN group and blocks all but one possible alternate link within the network. It can also be used as a Layer 2 redundancy or a load balancing mechanism for VLANs since MSTP can have different paths across different VLANs.

Figure 4-21 How MSTP works

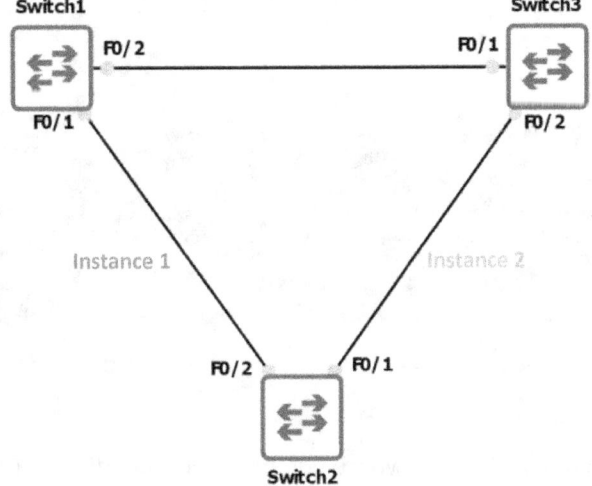

PVST		
Instance	VLANs	Root
8	5,10,15,20	Switch 1
	25,30,35,40	Switch 3

MSTP		
Instance	VLANs	Root
1	5,10,5,20	Switch 1
2	25,30,35,40	Switch 3

Let us consider the above figure. We assume that for this example, we have 8 different VLANs present on the network. What MSTP does, instead of creating 8 separate instances per VLAN, will reduce the number of cases and let the VLANs be grouped under these instances. The grouping process is called mapping. This means we can simply declare from Switch2, Instance 1 maps VLANs from 5 to 20, and for Instance 2 maps VLANs from 25 to 40.

Because of this, we have reduced the overhead of the switches since we only run 2 instances of STP, and we can also define load balancing where we can say Instance 1 has the primary root of Switch1, making the link from Switch1 to Switch2 as the forwarding path and link from Switch3 to Switch2 as its Blocked path, while for Instance 2 has the primary root of Switch 3 with its link going to Switch2 as the forwarding and link from Switch1 to Switch2 as the blocked one. See below figure.

Figure 4-22 Two Instances of MSTP

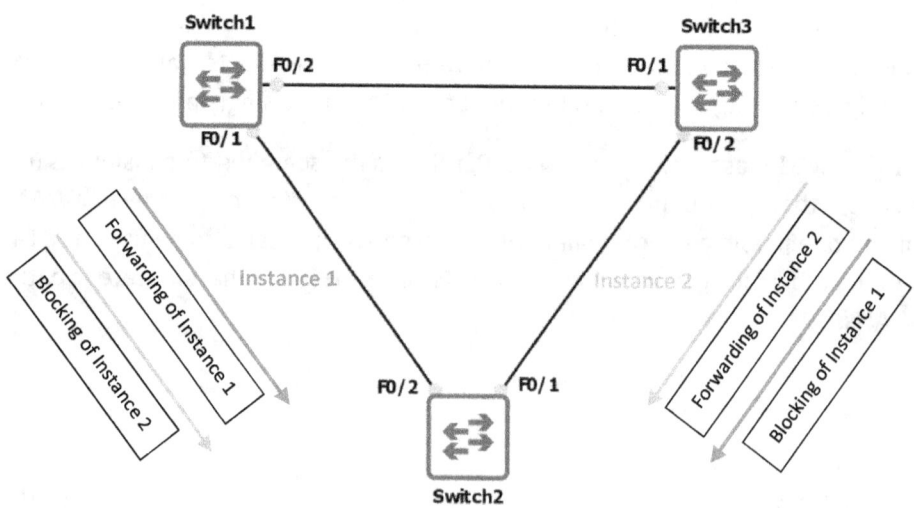

Terminology:

MSTP Instance – Is a process in STP which identifies a root bridge and different port roles for a group of switches that can be shared by multiple VLANs.

When to Use MSTP

Commonly, MSTP is used in a network setup where you have multiple VLANs. This could mean that the design of the network is somehow an enterprise where you have lots of areas or buildings, which then you need to configure trunking between those areas or buildings. Because of this, VLANs that appear from one area may go to another area. And this is where MSTP is recommended when switches have multiple VLANs on it.

MSTP Region

A unique trait of MSTP is it works in a group called region that permits a group of switches to be identified as a single bridge that shares attributes such as:

- The region name is a sensitive 32 bytes character combined with revision number used as a unique identifier for MSTP region.
- Revision number – is 2 bytes in combination with the region name used as an identifier for MSTP region. The range is from 0 to 65,535.
- VLAN mapping table – This contains the number of instances created and the VLANs associated with each instance. Breaks into:
    - Instance ID – Identifier, for example, the range is from 0 to 4094
    - VLAN range – number of VLANS to be associated per instance. The range is from 1 to 4094.

This region includes multiple spanning-tree instances (MSTI). According to Cisco, each VLAN is mapped to an MSTI, and for the devices to be in the same region, they must have the same VLANs to MSTIs mapping. The figure below shows how a region looks like.

Figure 4-22 MSTP Region

Region Name	MSU	
Revision Number	1	
	Instance	
VLAN Mapping	1	1-10
	2	11-20

For the above example, we assume that there are 20 VLANs available on the network; we set SW2, SW3, SW5, and SW6 running as MSTP and be members of the region. Since they are now within the region, they should share attributes.

> **Note:**
> Unlike, VTP where changes made from one switch is automatically propagated to other switches, in MSTP if you want to associate a VLAN to specific instance, you need to manually enter it on each switch. Same goes with the revision number. Switches within the region also do not exchange the entire mapping table, what it does is it uses a hashing algorithm on the table and sends the hash result to other switches within the region which will then be executed by the switch and it compares the hash to their own table. If the hash is matched then the switch concludes they have matched mapping tables, else it would think it's a boundary of the region from another region.

MSTP Configuration

For the configuration of MSTP, let us consider the below topology as our guide.

Figure 4-23 MSTP Region

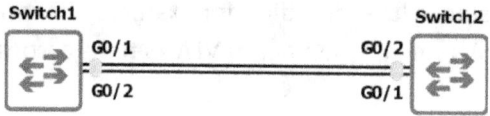

VLANs 5, 10, 15, and 20

We will assume for this given network that we have four (4) VLANs. We want to create 2 instances where VLANs 5 and 10 belong to the first instance, and VLANs 15 and 20 under the second instance wherein instance 1's primary root is Switch1, and Instance 2's primary root is Switch2. Below is the configuration needed to achieve the desired output.

Command	Description	
`SwitchX>en`	Moves to privilege mode	
`SwitchX#config t`	Moves to Global configuration mode	
`SwitchX(config)#spanning-tree mode mst`	Enables MSTP	
`SwitchX(config)#spanning-tree mst config`	Moves to MST configuration mode	
`SwitchX(config-mst)#name MSU`	Sets region name to MSU	
`SwitchX(config-mst)#revision 1`	Set revision number to 1	
`SwitchX(config-mst)#instance 1 VLAN 5,10`	VLAN mapping for instance 1	*Note: In case the VLAN IDs are in order you can declare for example instance 1 VLAN 1-5*
`SwitchX(config-mst)#instance 2 VLAN 15,20`	VLAN mapping for instance 2	

MSTP Election

To set Switch1 as Root Bridge for instance 1, and Switch2 as Root Bridge for instance 2, use the following commands:

Switch1	
`Switch1>`**`en`**	Moves to privilege mode
`Switch1#`**`config t`**	Moves to Global configuration mode
`Switch1(config)#`**`spanning-tree mst 1 root primary`**	Set instance 1 as root bridge with a priority value of 24,576
`Switch1(config)#`**`spanning-tree mst 2 root secondary`**	Set instance 2 as a secondary bridge with a priority value of 28,672

Switch2	
`Switch2>`**`en`**	Moves to privilege mode
`Switch2#`**`config t`**	Moves to Global configuration mode
`Switch2(config)#`**`spanning-tree mst 2 root primary`**	Set instance 2 as root bridge with a priority value of 24,576
`Switch2(config)#`**`spanning-tree mst 1 root secondary`**	Set instance 1 as a secondary bridge with a priority value of 28,672

Another alternative way to set the Root bridge per instance is by declaring the Priority value instead of the word feature. Below are the commands used:

Switch1	
`Switch1>`**`en`**	Moves to privilege mode
`Switch1#`**`config t`**	Moves to Global configuration mode
`Switch1(config)#`**`spanning-tree mst 1 priority 0`**	Set instance 1 as root bridge with a priority value of 0
`Switch1(config)#`**`spanning-tree mst 2 priority 4096`**	Set instance 2 as a secondary bridge with a priority value of 4096

Switch2	
`Switch2>`**`en`**	Moves to privilege mode
`Switch2#`**`config t`**	Moves to Global configuration mode
`Switch2(config)#`**`spanning-tree mst 2 priority 0`**	Set instance 2 as root bridge with a priority value of 0
`Switch2(config)#`**`spanning-tree mst 1 priority 4096`**	Set instance 1 as a secondary bridge with a priority value of 4096

MSTP Port Priority Configuration

This is used especially when a loop occurs and when the MSTP needs to select a port to put into the forwarding state. To assign a higher or lower priority value manually to ports, use the following commands:

`SwitchX>`**`en`**	Moves to privilege mode
`SwitchX#`**`config t`**	Moves to Global configuration mode
`SwitchX(config)#`**`interface g0/1`**	Enters to interface configuration mode of g0/1
`SwitchX(config-if)#`**`spanning-tree mst 1 port-priority 1`**	Set port priority of g0/1 to 1; for instance, 1 Range is from 0 to 240 and is increment by 240. To declare port-priority to multiple Instances, you can declare the 1st instance-id followed by hyphen up to the desired target instance.

MSTP Path Cost Configuration

To manually set path cost value, use the below commands.

`SwitchX>`**`en`**	Moves to privilege mode
`SwitchX#`**`config t`**	Moves to Global configuration mode
`SwitchX(config)#`**`interface g0/1`**	Enters to interface configuration mode of g0/1
`SwitchX(config-if)#`**`spanning-tree mst 1 cost 1`**	Set path cost for g0/1 instance 1 to 1. The default path cost is based on the media speed of the interface. Range for path cost configuration is from 1 to 200000000.

MSTP Hello Time Configuration

This is used to change the interval between the generation of config messages by the Root Bridge. Below are the commands.

`SwitchX>`**`en`**	Moves to privilege mode
`SwitchX#`**`config t`**	Moves to Global configuration mode
`SwitchX(config)#`**`spanning-tree mst hello-time 10`**	Set hello time to 10 seconds. The default value is 2. Choices for the interval are from 1 to 10.

MSTP Forwarding-Delay Time Configuration

You can manually set the forward delay time for all MST instances. The forward delay is the period of how long a port should wait before changing from the spanning-tree learning and listening states to the forwarding state.

`SwitchX>`**`en`**	Moves to privilege mode
`SwitchX#`**`config t`**	Moves to Global configuration mode
`SwitchX(config)#`**`spanning-tree mst forward-time 4`**	Set forward delay time to 4 seconds. Default value is 15, but you can choose from the range of 4 to 30 seconds.

MSTP Max Aging Time Configuration

To set the max-aging time for all instances of MSTP manually, use the following commands. Max-aging time is the number of periods in which the switch should wait without receiving spanning-tree config messages before establishing a reconfiguration.

`SwitchX>`**`en`**	Moves to privilege mode
`SwitchX#`**`config t`**	Moves to Global configuration mode
`SwitchX(config)#`**`spanning-tree mst max-age 6`**	Set max-aging time to 6 seconds. The default value is 20, but can be changed from 6 to 40 seconds.

MSTP Max-Hop Count Configuration

This is used to specify the number of hops in a region before BDPU is discarded and the port's aging information.

`SwitchX>`**`en`**	Moves to privilege mode
`SwitchX#`**`config t`**	Moves to Global configuration mode
`SwitchX(config)#`**`spanning-tree mst max-hops 10`**	Set hop-count to 10. Available options are from 1 to 255. The default value is 20.

Verifying MST

Used the following command to verify MST status and configuration

`SwitchX>`**`en`**	Moves to privilege mode
`SwitchX#`**`show spanning-tree mst configuration`**	Shows the MST region configuration
`SwitchX#`**`show spanning-tree mst configuration digest`**	Shows the MD5 digest

`SwitchX#show spanning-tree mst [instance id]`	Shows the MST information for a specific Instance
`SwitchX#show spanning-tree mst interface [interface-id]`	Shows MST information for a specific Instance

Let us consider the previous example we had when applying the above commands; this is how MST information looks like.

```
Switch 1
Switch1#show spanning-tree mst config
Name        [MSU]
Revision  1          Instances configured 3

Instance  VLANs mapped
--------  ----------------------------------------------------------------
0         1-4,6-9,11-14,16-19,21-4094
1         5,10
2         15,20


Switch1#show spanning-tree mst config digest
Name        [MSU]
Revision  1          Instances configured 3
Digest              0x31C76491AF2413F2836B31560EFDC98E
Pre-std Digest      0x6DD365308CEE09DB9EF4F78EF10D0F3B

Switch1#show spanning-tree mst 1

##### MST1    VLANs mapped:   5,10
Bridge        address 5000.0001.0000  priority    1     (0 sysid 1)
Root          this switch for MST1

Interface        Role Sts Cost      Prio.Nbr Type
---------------- ---- --- --------- -------- --------------------------
Gi0/1            Desg FWD 20000     128.2    P2p
Gi0/2            Desg FWD 20000     128.3    P2p

Switch1#show spanning-tree mst 2

##### MST2    VLANs mapped:   15,20
Bridge        address 5000.0001.0000  priority    4098  (4096 sysid 2)
Root          address 5000.0002.0000  priority    2     (0 sysid 2)
              port    Gi0/2            cost       20000    rem hops 19

Interface        Role Sts Cost      Prio.Nbr Type
---------------- ---- --- --------- -------- --------------------------
Gi0/1            Altn BLK 20000     128.2    P2p
Gi0/2            Root FWD 20000     128.3    P2p

Switch1#show spanning-tree mst interface g0/1

GigabitEthernet0/1 of MST0 is designated forwarding
```

```
Portfast : no              (default)      port guard : none     (default)
Link type: point-to-point  (auto)         bpdu filter: disable (default)
Boundary : internal                       bpdu guard : disable (default)
PVST Sim : enable          (default)
Bpdus sent 278, received 256

Instance Role Sts Cost      Prio.Nbr VLANs mapped
-------- ---- --- --------- -------- -------------------------------
0        Desg FWD 20000     128.2    1-4,6-9,11-14,16-19,21-4094
1        Desg FWD 20000     128.2    5,10
2        Altn BLK 20000     128.2    15,20

Switch1#show spanning-tree mst interface g0/2

GigabitEthernet0/2 of MST0 is designated forwarding
Portfast : no              (default)      port guard : none     (default)
Link type: point-to-point  (auto)         bpdu filter: disable (default)
Boundary : internal                       bpdu guard : disable (default)
PVST Sim : enable          (default)
Bpdus sent 283, received 254

Instance Role Sts Cost      Prio.Nbr VLANs mapped
-------- ---- --- --------- -------- -------------------------------
0        Desg FWD 20000     128.3    1-4,6-9,11-14,16-19,21-4094
1        Desg FWD 20000     128.3    5,10
2        Root FWD 20000     128.3    15,20
```

Switch 2

```
Switch2#show spanning-tree mst config
Name       [MSU]
Revision   1       Instances configured 3

Instance   VLANs mapped
--------   ---------------------------------------------------------
0          1-4,6-9,11-14,16-19,21-4094
1          5,10
2          15,20
--------   ---------------------------------------------------------

Switch2#show spanning-tree mst config digest
Name       [MSU]
Revision   1       Instances configured 3
Digest             0x31C76491AF2413F2836B31560EFDC98E
Pre-std Digest     0x6DD365308CEE09DB9EF4F78EF10D0F3B

Switch2#show spanning-tree mst 1

##### MST1    VLANs mapped:  5,10
Bridge        address 5000.0002.0000  priority   4097  (4096 sysid 1)
Root          address 5000.0001.0000  priority   1     (0 sysid 1)
              port    Gi0/2           cost       20000     rem hops 19
```

```
Interface           Role Sts Cost      Prio.Nbr Type
------------------- ---- --- --------- -------- --------------------------------
Gi0/1               Altn BLK 20000     128.2    P2p
Gi0/2               Root FWD 20000     128.3    P2p

Switch2#show spanning-tree mst 2

##### MST2     VLANs mapped:   15,20
Bridge         address 5000.0002.0000  priority    2    (0 sysid 2)
Root           this switch for MST2

Interface           Role Sts Cost      Prio.Nbr Type
------------------- ---- --- --------- -------- --------------------------------
Gi0/1               Desg FWD 20000     128.2    P2p
Gi0/2               Desg FWD 20000     128.3    P2p


Switch2#show spanning-tree mst interface g0/1

GigabitEthernet0/1 of MST0 is alternate blocking
Portfast : no               (default)      port guard : none     (default)
Link type: point-to-point (auto)           bpdu filter: disable  (default)
Boundary : internal                        bpdu guard : disable  (default)
PVST Sim : enable           (default)
Bpdus sent 469, received 476

Instance Role Sts Cost      Prio.Nbr VLANs mapped
-------- ---- --- --------- -------- -------------------------------
0        Altn BLK 20000     128.2    1-4,6-9,11-14,16-19,21-4094
1        Altn BLK 20000     128.2    5,10
2        Desg FWD 20000     128.2    15,20

Switch2#show spanning-tree mst interface g0/2

GigabitEthernet0/2 of MST0 is root forwarding
Portfast : no               (default)      port guard : none     (default)
Link type: point-to-point (auto)           bpdu filter: disable  (default)
Boundary : internal                        bpdu guard : disable  (default)
PVST Sim : enable           (default)
Bpdus sent 500, received 500

Instance Role Sts Cost      Prio.Nbr VLANs mapped
-------- ---- --- --------- -------- -------------------------------
0        Root FWD 20000     128.3    1-4,6-9,11-14,16-19,21-4094
1        Root FWD 20000     128.3    5,10
2        Desg FWD 20000     128.3    15,20
```

Virtual Local Area Network

CHAPTER 5

Flat Network

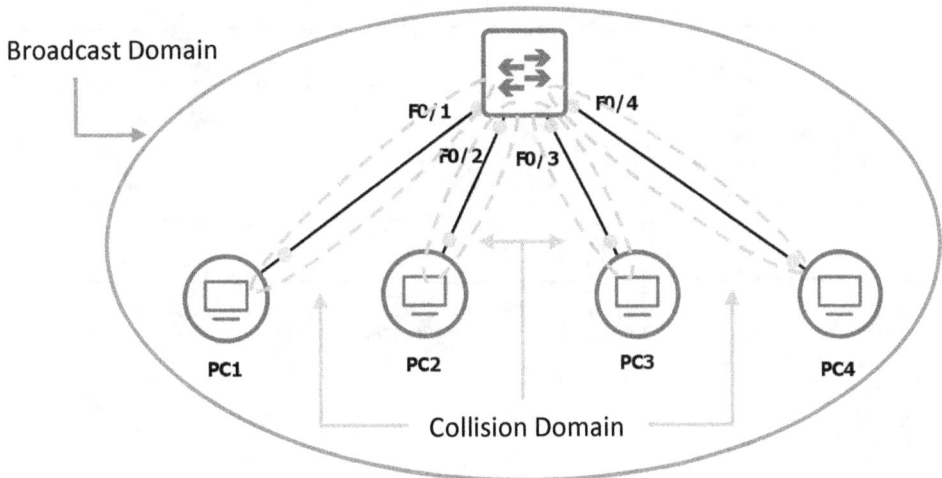

Figure 5-1

Technically, a layer-2 switched network is a flat network, where all segments belong to a single broadcast domain but has a separate collision domain since it is based per segment *(switches run in the full-duplex mode)*. It can be compared to a flat land-field where all houses located in that area can see each other and belongs to a single compound, village, or a barangay

Security issues may arise within a flat network for all users to see all connected devices. This is very dangerous, especially to an organization where IT or network administrator handling their network are not that techy, which means if an intruder connects his device to the switch (having the switch with no security configuration), the attacker can scan and see all connected devices/ users including those servers that are prohibited from being accessed by anyone.

In a flat network, the same group of devices should also be placed within one geographical location. Refer to the next page figure.

Figure 5-2

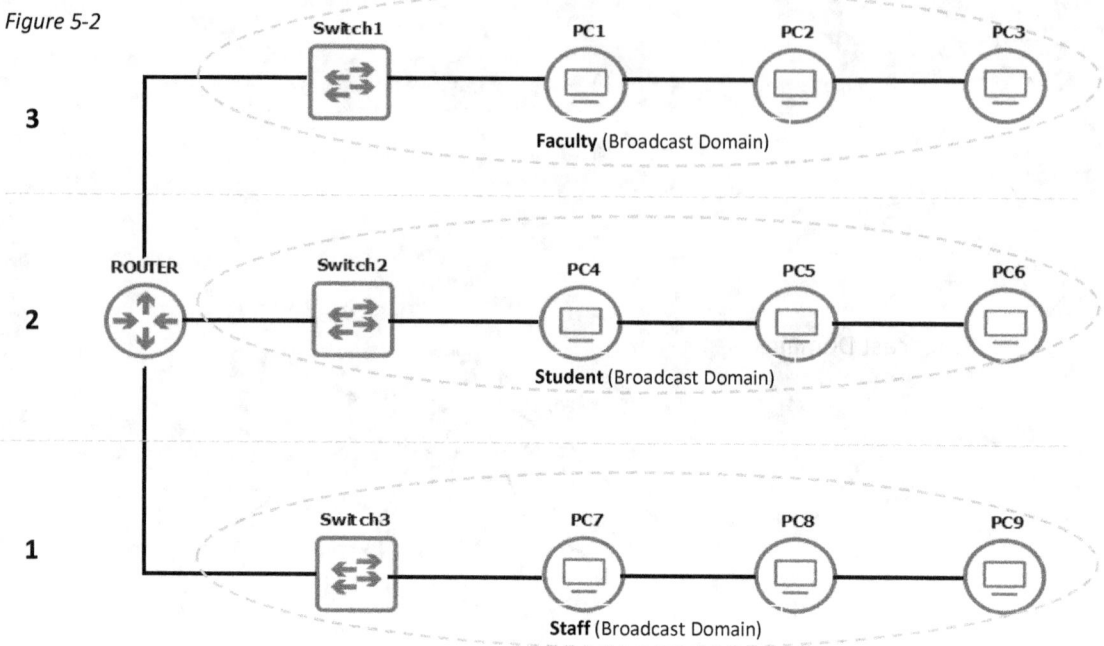

Figure 5-2 shows a network of a 3-story building of a school. There are 3 groups within the building which are then grouped into switches per level. A flat network limits the placement of devices to a single area only and is connected to the same equipment since each group should share the same subnet and broadcast domain.

Virtual Local Area Network (802.1Q)

In a traditional LAN network, we have discussed from the previous topic that it can be referred to as a flat network where devices connected to the same equipment share broadcast domain. With VLAN integration in the network, you can segregate and minimize the broadcast domain by breaking it into smaller parts, meaning that broadcast from other subnetwork should remain only within its vicinity and not affect other subnetworks.

Let us consider our previous network topology in figure 5-2. We can distribute groups to other levels using VLAN even though they are not connected to the same equipment.

Figure 5-3

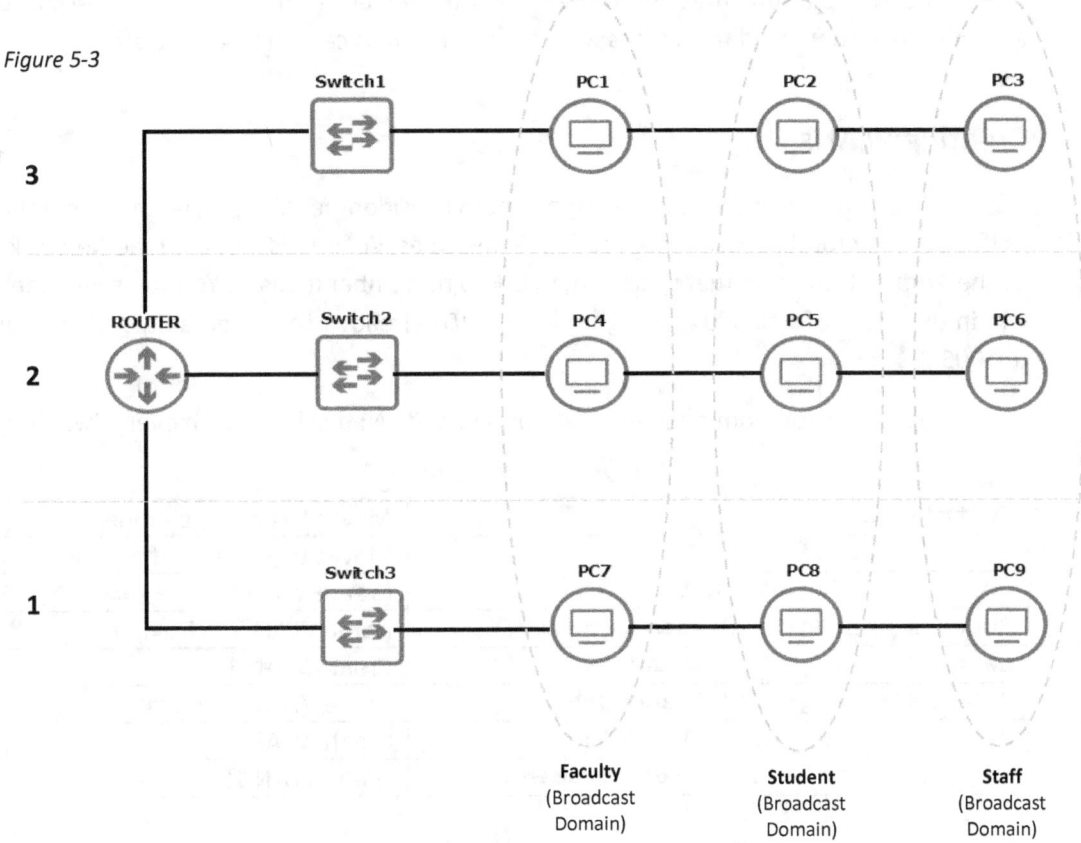

A Virtual Local Area Network is a logical grouping of users, which means they may seem physically connected to a single device, but virtually they are separated. In VLAN, we create multiple logical networks within one network, thus breaking the broadcast domain into smaller parts. With VLAN, associating devices to groups is no longer limited to the physical location.

Two Major Functions

There are two major functions that the VLAN can do:

- Each VLAN contains broadcast
- VLAN groups devices. Devices that are members of other VLANs can never be seen by other VLANs (except when firewall configuration is created allowing them to be seen or using and Inter-VLAN routing).

Management VLAN

Every network has its management VLAN ready. The management VLAN, by default, is the VLAN 1. This is where we used to assign IP for the switch to configure the device remotely. Moreover, it is also used to exchange information with other network devices.

VLAN 1 is also named the Native VLAN by default. Native VLAN is a special VLAN that accommodates untagged traffic. It is where the trunk links carry untagged traffic.

Creating VLANs

To create or add a VLAN, it is important to consider the VLAN ID and the Name that serves as the identifier for that VLAN organization. Sometimes, VLAN ID is based on the Network Address by the Administrators for that specific network to remember it easily. You can select the VLAN ID within the range of 1 to 4094, though there are IDs already used by default, such as 1 and 1002 to 1005.

Use the below command to create or add a VLAN; this is done on every Switch.

Command	Description
`SwitchX>en`	Moves to privilege mode
`SwitchX#config t`	Moves to global configuration mode
`SwitchX(config)#VLAN 5`	Create VLAN 5
`SwitchX(config-VLAN)#name Faculty`	Name VLAN 5 to Faculty
`SwitchX(config-VLAN)#VLAN 10`	Create VLAN 10
`SwitchX(config-VLAN)#name Staff`	Name VLAN 10 to Staff
`SwitchX(config-VLAN)#VLAN 15`	Create VLAN 15
`SwitchX(config-VLAN)#name Student`	Name VLAN 15 to Student

Do delete VLANs; issue the command **"no VLAN *VLAN-id*"** in the global configuration mode.

Benefits of VLAN

Below are the benefits of integrating VLAN configuration in your network.

Limits Broadcast

With VLAN, you can control the broadcast that propagates within the network. Broadcast is received only by devices members of a specific VLAN even though these devices are connected to the same network equipment. Broadcast does not forward to other VLANs; thus, it is only contained within that particular VLAN.

Security Control

With VLAN, users are separated and control what devices can talk to another host since each VLAN functions as a separate LAN. This is executed since administrators are now given the privilege to control each port and user, thereby limiting unnecessary connections to be established once a user plugs his device to the switch since ports are now managed, and resources are regulated.

Easy Management

Network administrators are given the power to organize the network logically instead of physically.

Flexibility and Scalability

Workstations can now be moved freely without reconfiguring the whole network, and switches running VLAN is adaptable to expansions. Adding users is easily done regardless of their physical location. With VLAN, you can save more since additional hardware and cabling are no more necessary.

VLAN Memberships

To associate a port to a particular VLAN ID, we used the VLAN Membership configuration. There are two common ways of assigning ports to a specific VLAN.

Static VLAN

This is the typical way of assigning ports to a VLAN but is the most secured. The administrator configures the assignment; because of this, it is easy for the administrator to monitor the user's movement within the network.

Use the commands to assign the port to a VLAN.

`SwitchX>`**`en`**	Moves to privilege mode
`SwitchX#`**`config t`**	Moves to global configuration mode
`SwitchX(config)#`**`int f0/1`**	Moves to interface configuration mode for f0/1
`SwitchX(config-if)#`**`switchport access VLAN 5`**	Assign f0/1 to VLAN 5
`SwitchX(config-if)#`**`int f0/2`**	Moves to interface configuration mode for f0/2
`SwitchX(config-if)#`**`switchport access VLAN 10`**	Assign f0/2 to VLAN 10
`SwitchX(config-if)#`**`int f0/3`**	Moves to interface configuration mode for f0/3
`SwitchX(config-if)#`**`switchport access VLAN 15`**	Assign f0/3 to VLAN 15

Dynamic VLAN

In this method, a port is assigned to a particular VLAN ID automatically. This requires a VLAN Membership Policy Server (VMPS), a centralized server that selects what VLAN should a port be assigned, and this is done dynamically and based on the MAC address of the device connected to the port. There are only limited cisco switch models that can run VMPS; models that can run VMPS are Cisco Catalyst 4500 series and 6500 series running Catalyst Operating System.

VMPS uses UDP port to listen to VQP (VLAN Query Protocol) requests from the clients. Clients do not need to know whether the VMPS resides locally or remotely. When the VMPS receives a request from the client, it will search its database for an entry of a MAC Address to VLAN mapping *(www.cisco.com)*.

Once the VMPS receives the request, it will take one action from the following options:

- If the VLAN ID assigned to the requesting client is restricted to a group of ports, the server will verify the requesting port from this group and will answer as follows:

  - The VLAN name is sent to the client if the VLAN is allowed on the port.
  - If it is not allowed and the VMPS is not in secure mode, the server will respond to the client that the access is denied
  - If it is not allowed, but the VMPS is in secure mode, the server will respond to the client a port shutdown.

- Suppose the entry on the database does not match the existing VLAN on the port, and there are active users or hosts on the port. In that case, the server sends an "access denied" (open), a "fallback VLAN name" (open with fallback VLAN configured), a "port-shutdown" (secure), or a "new VLAN name" (multiple) responses, depending on the secure mode setting of the VMPS *(www.cisco.com)*.

> **Note:**
> *For this book, we will not cover the configuration of dynamic vlan membership*

Voice VLAN

This is a special VLAN membership intended only for VoIP devices. To assign port as voice, use the following commands:

`SwitchX>`**`en`**	Moves to privilege mode
`SwitchX#`**`config t`**	Moves to global configuration mode
`SwitchX(config)#`**`int f0/1`**	Moves to interface configuration mode for f0/1
`SwitchX(config-if)#`**`switchport mode access`**	Set f0/1 as Access link

`SwitchX(config-if)#switchport voice VLAN 1`	Set f0/1 as Voice VLAN under VLAN 1

Switching Link Types

It is very important to identify link types used in the switching configuration. This link type determines whether a connection is capable of handling multiple VLANs or not.

1. Access Link

These are links that are part of one VLAN referred to as the native VLAN of the port. Devices that are then attached to this type of link are not aware of the VLAN Membership. This link carries only untagged packets, which means the switch removes the VLAN information before passing the frame to the access device connected on it.

Devices that are part of this link cannot communicate with other devices that are no longer part of their VLAN unless the packet is routed through a router. Usually, this is configured to ports that connect the switch to the PC.

`SwitchX>en`	Moves to privilege mode
`SwitchX#config t`	Moves to global configuration mode
`SwitchX(config)#int f0/1`	Moves to interface configuration mode for f0/1
`SwitchX(config-if)#switchport mode access`	Set f0/1 as Access link

Note: You can also use port ranging if multiple ports are configured with the same content.

2. Trunk Link

Links that are point-to-point connection for switch to switch, switch to a router or sometimes switch to a server is referred to as Trunk link. Trunk links are capable of carrying multiple VLANs. The trunk can be configured as to how many VLANs can pass through within its link. When multiple VLANs are traveling across the same link, VLAN ID is tagged and added into the frame.

Configuration for trunk links differs per OS. For Cisco IOS software, which is commonly available for 2960 series switches, use the following command to configure the trunk link.

`SwitchX>`**`en`**	Moves to privilege mode
`SwitchX#`**`config t`**	Moves to global configuration mode
`SwitchX(config)#`**`int g0/1`**	Moves to interface configuration mode for g0/1
`SwitchX(config-if)#`**`switchport mode trunk`**	Set g0/1 as Trunk link

For switches running Catalyst OS, use the following commands:

`SwitchX>`**`en`**	Moves to privilege mode
`SwitchX#`**`config t`**	Moves to global configuration mode
`SwitchX(config)#`**`int g0/1`**	Moves to interface configuration mode for f0/1
`SwitchX(config-if)#`**`switchport trunk encapsulation dot1q`** Or `SwitchX(config-if)#`**`switchport trunk encapsulation isl`**	Designate port as trunk and define encapsulation as either ISL or 802.1q (dot1q)
`SwitchX(config-if)#`**`switchport mode trunk`**	Set g0/1 as Trunk link
`SwitchX(config-if)#`**`switchport trunk native VLAN 5`**	Set native VLAN of untagged frames to VLAN 5
`SwitchX(config-if)#`**`switchport trunk allowed VLAN 1-15`**	Allows VLAN 1 to 15 to travel across the trunk link

To remove the commands, just issue the word **"no"** at the beginning of the command.

To verify ports. Issue the following commands:

`SwitchX>`**`en`**	Moves to privilege mode
`SwitchX#`**`show interface g0/1 switchport`**	Shows switchport status of interface g0/1

How VLAN Works

Keeping track of users in the switched environment is very important, especially when VLAN is implemented. How VLAN keeps track of its connected clients is observed by using the technique of frame tagging.

Frame tagging is the process of marking the user by adding a unique ID and header known as VLAN identification header to its frame as it travels across switches and VLANs. The frame tagging was introduced by Cisco when an Ethernet frame crosses a trunk link. All switches where the frame took its path must identify the VLAN ID associated with it. Whenever the frame arrives at a switch that has another trunked link, the frame will be forwarded out to that trunk link port until such time that when the frame reaches an exit to an access link port, the VLAN ID will now be removed by the switch.

Figure 5-4. Frame with VLAN ID Header

Dst. Mac	Src. Mac	Type/ Length	Data	FCS

Dst. Mac	Src. Mac	Tag	Type/ Length	Data	FCS

Type (0x8100)	Pri	CFI	VID
2 Bytes	3 Bits	1 Bit	12 Bits

Introduction to Dynamic Trunking Protocol

Dynamic Trunking Protocol (DTP) is a Cisco proprietary protocol made for trunking negotiation and the type of encapsulation to be used between VLAN-aware switches.

The following points characterize the DTP:

- It is on by default on Cisco 2960 and 2950 catalyst switches
- The Dynamic-auto mode is on by default on 2950 and 2960 Cisco switches
- Can be turned off using the command **nonegotiate**
- Can be turned on using the **dynamic-auto** command
- To avoid negotiation issues in the commands of **switchport mode trunk** and **switchport mode access**, set the switch to a static trunk or static access

SwitchX>**en**	Moves to privilege mode
SwitchX#**config t**	Moves to global configuration mode

`SwitchX(config)#int g0/1`	Moves to interface configuration mode for f0/1
`SwitchX(config-if)#switchport mode trunk`	Set g0/1 as Trunk link
`SwitchX(config-if)#switchport nonegotiate`	Prevents the specific interface in generating DTP frames

Below are the configuration options for DTP

	Dynamic Auto	Dynamic Desirable	Trunk	Access
Dynamic Auto	Access	Trunk	Trunk	Access
Dynamic Desirable	Trunk	Trunk	Trunk	Access
Trunk	Trunk	Trunk	Trunk	Limited connectivity
Access	Access	Access	Limited connectivity	Access

`SwitchX>en`	Moves to privilege mode
`SwitchX#config t`	Moves to global configuration mode
`SwitchX(config)#int g0/1`	Moves to interface configuration mode for f0/1
`SwitchX(config-if)#switchport mode dynamic desirable`	It makes the interface actively attempt to convert the link to a trunk link
`SwitchX(config-if)#switchport mode dynamic auto`	Set the interface able to convert into a trunk link

To verify DTP mode currently configured on an interface, use the command **show dtp interface** *int-no.*

> **Note:**
>
> *As best practice in the field, it is recommended to turnoff DTP*

VLAN Trunking Protocol

CHAPTER 6

You are a company's network administrator based in a hundred-story building with at least one switch per floor. Isn't it challenging to configure those switches one by one, especially when creating VLANs or modifying the VLANs across the network? Well, you are lucky enough if those switches are Cisco switches. With the help of VTP or the VLAN Trunking Protocol, changes to VLANs registered on a switch will be easier to be advertised to other neighboring switches connected within the network.

Cisco created this protocol for the administrator to easily manage all configured VLANs across the switched network and maintain consistency all over the network. With VTP, this allows the administrator to make changes whether to add, delete, and rename VLAN names which are then propagated to all switches.

The following are the benefits of VTP to a switched network:

- Consistent configuration of VLAN in all switches in the network
- Allows the VLANs to be trunked over mixed networks
- Tracking and monitoring of VLAN is accurate
- Reporting of added VLANs to all switches is dynamic
- VLAN adding is plug and play

VTP Modes

VTP modes are identified into three operations.

Figure 6-1. Frame with VLAN ID Header

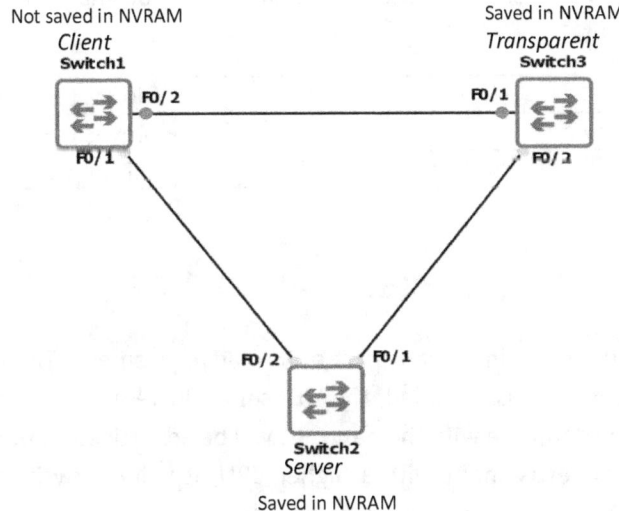

95

- **Server** – all Cisco catalyst switches are by default configured as VTP Server. A server is important and needed to propagate VLAN information throughout the area of switched network. With server mode, the administrator can add and delete VLANs in a VTP domain. Any changes or alteration made in the server switch is automatically advertising to the entire VTP domain. The best practice is to configure the VTP mode server on the switch directly connected from the router.

`SwitchX>`**`en`**	Moves to privilege mode
`SwitchX#`**`config t`**	Moves to global configuration mode
`SwitchX(config)#`**`vtp mode server`**	Set the switch as VTP server
`SwitchX(config)#`**`vtp domain`** `domain-name`	Set VTP domain name, which is 1 to 32 characters long.
`SwitchX(config)#`**`vtp password`** `password`	Set VTP Password
`SwitchX(config)#`**`vtp v2-mode`**	Sets the VTP version to 2. All switches must share the same version.

- **Client** – Switches configured as a client will just have to receive and send updated information coming from the VTP server but cannot make any changes.

`SwitchX>`**`en`**	Moves to privilege mode
`SwitchX#`**`config t`**	Moves to global configuration mode
`SwitchX(config)#`**`vtp mode client`**	Set the switch as VTP client

- **Transparent** – Switches in transparent mode do not participate in the VTP domain but will forward VTP advertisements using the trunk link ports. The administrator can add and delete VLANs under this mode since the switch running transparent keeps its database and does not share it with other switches; for that reason, it is considered locally significant.

`SwitchX>`**`en`**	Moves to privilege mode
`SwitchX#`**`config t`**	Moves to global configuration mode
`SwitchX(config)#`**`vtp mode server`**	Set the switch as VTP transparent

Configuration Revision Number

This is the most important part of VTP advertisement. The operation governing CRN is that once the database is modified, the VTP server increments the revision number by 1. After that, the updated database with the new CRN will be advertised by the VTP server. When switches can receive an advertisement with a higher CRN, it will overwrite the database stored in the NVRAM with the updated one being advertised.

The increment of CRN can be done on every switch by adding a VLAN.

VTP Pruning

VTP Pruning reduces the amount of broadcast, multicasts, and other unicast packets, which in return preserves and saves bandwidth when configuring VTP. The beauty of pruning is that it only sends the broadcast to trunk links that need the information, and those who don't will receive them.

`SwitchX>`**`en`**	Moves to privilege mode
`SwitchX#`**`config t`**	Moves to global configuration mode
`SwitchX(config)#`**`vtp pruning`**	Enables VTP Pruning

Note:

All switches are by default sets the vtp pruning to disabled. VTP Pruning must be enabled only on 1 switch operating as server mode.

Inter-VLAN Communication

CHAPTER 7

Recall from the previous chapter that every user in the network associated with a specific VLAN identification is by default cannot communicate with users of different VLAN associations since they are in different broadcast domains. But, what if a company is required to separate the users by VLAN, but they should be able to communicate with each other?

In this section, we will discuss the operation of Inter-VLAN communication.

Inter-VLAN Routing Operation

This operation is the process of forwarding network traffic from one VLAN to another VLAN. Inter-VLAN routing enables the user of different VLAN membership to communicate with other users associated with other VLAN.

There are there common Inter-VLAN routing operations used in the field:

- Legacy Inter-VLAN routing
- Router-on-a-Stick
- Layer 3 Switch by the use of Switched Virtual Interfaces (SVI)

LEGACY INTER-VLAN ROUTING

This was the first introduced solution that uses a router of multiple Ethernet interfaces. In the legacy operation, each Ethernet interface of the router is connected to the switch and is membered to a different VLAN identification. The active Interfaces of the router connected to the switch serve as the port for the default gateway of each VLANs associated.

Figure 7-1. Frame with VLAN ID Header

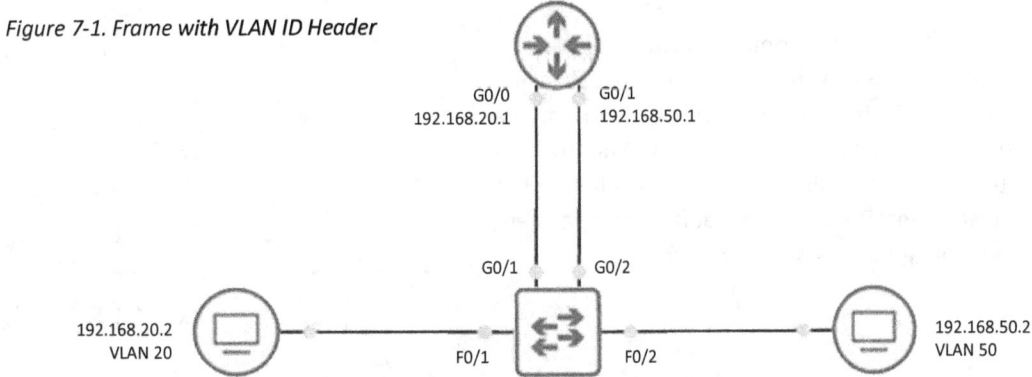

With this type of operation, it presents a significant limitation for it disregards the concept of scalability. Our routers have limited physical Ethernet interfaces, which in return limits the number of VLANs that can be created on the network. Also, the need for interfaces that will serve each VLAN quickly exhaust a router's hardware interface capacity.

With this operation's mentioned limitations and downsides, the legacy Inter-VLAN routing is no longer implemented in switched networks.

Router-on-a-Stick Inter-VLAN Routing

This operation overcomes and solves the limitation of the legacy Inter-VLAN routing. Unlike the legacy, Router-on-a-Stick uses only one physical Ethernet interface to route traffic between the VLANs existing on the network. According to theory, the Router-on-a-stick supports only a maximum of 50 VLANs on the network.

The following are the guiding points for configuring this routing operation:

- The router's interface should be configured as an 802.1Q and connected to a switch's trunk port.
- The sub-interfaces to be configured are all virtual interfaces that are associated with a single physical Ethernet interface.
- The sub-interfaces to be created must match with the existing and created VLAN ID assignment on the network.
- Unlike the traditional assignment of IPs on the interface, each subinterface is configured with a unique gateway under a different subnet.
- Every VLAN-tagged traffic that crosses the router's interface is forwarded to the sub-interface that matches its tagged VLAN ID.
- After that, the router will have to decide and route the traffic to the exit interface based on the destination IP network address.
- An exit interface configured as an 802.1Q sub-interface will have its data frames be VLAN-tagged with the new VLAN and sent back out to the physical interface.

Example:

A network is configured with 2 Vlans. PC 1 is associated with Vlan 5 while PC 2 is associated with Vlan 10. The link between the router and the switch is configured as trunk link. The router's interface to the switch is in 802.1Q. All switches management IP stays on the default management Vlan. Configure Inter-Vlan communication

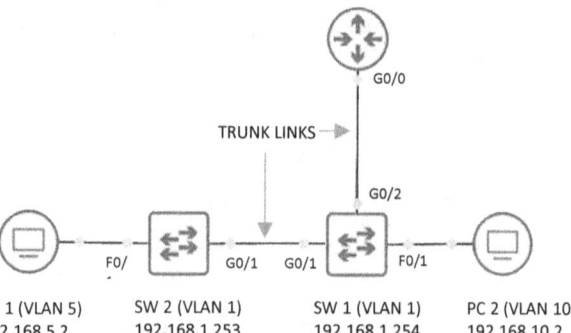

CONFIGURATION STEPS:

For the devices on the figure to communicate with each other, the following configuration is needed.

At Switch 1

Sw1>**en**	Moves to privilege mode
Sw1#**config t**	Moves to global configuration mode
Sw1(config)#**vtp mode server**	Set the switch as VTP server
Sw1(config)#**vtp domain msu**	Set VTP domain to MSU
Sw1(config)#**VLAN 5**	Creates VLAN 5
Sw1(config-VLAN)#**name LAN5**	Set name of VLAN 5 to LAN5
Sw1(config-VLAN)#**exit**	Return to Global configuration mode
Sw1(config)#**VLAN 10**	Creates VLAN 10
Sw1(config-VLAN)#**name LAN10**	Set name of VLAN 10 to LAN10
Sw1(config-VLAN)#**exit**	Returns to global configuration mode
Sw1(config)#**interface VLAN 1**	Open management VLAN
Sw1(config-if)#**ip add 192.168.1.254 255.255.255.0**	Assigns IP Address of 192.168.1.254 to switch with a subnet mask of 255.255.255.0 in VLAN 1 for remote access
Sw1(config-if)#**no shut**	Enables the interface
Sw1(config-if)#**ip default-gateway 192.168.1.1**	Configure default gateway for the switch (Default Gateway is the IP Address of the Router)
Sw1(config)#**interface f0/1**	Moves to interface configuration mode
Sw1(config-if)#**switchport mode access**	Set f0/1 as Access link
Sw1(config-if)#**switchport access VLAN 10**	Assign f0/1 to VLAN 10
Sw1(config-if)#**no shut**	Enables the interface
Sw1(config-if)#**exit**	Returns to global configuration mode
Sw1(config)#**interface range g0/1-2**	Moves to interface configuration mode selecting two interfaces from g0/1 to g0/2
Sw1(config-if-range)#**switchport mode trunk**	Set g0/1 and g0/2 as Trunk link
Sw1(config-if-range)#**switchport trunk allowed VLAN 1,5,10**	Allows VLAN 1,5 and 10 to travel across the trunk link
Sw1(config-if-range)#**switchport nonegotiate**	Prevents the specific interface in generating DTP frames
Sw1(config-if-range)#**no shut**	Enables the interface(s)
Sw1(config-if-range)#**end**	Returns to privilege mode

At Switch 2

Command	Description
`Sw2>en`	Moves to privilege mode
`Sw2#config t`	Moves to global configuration mode
`Sw2(config)#vtp mode client`	Set the switch as VTP client
`Sw2(config)#vtp domain msu`	Set VTP domain to MSU
`Sw2(config)#interface VLAN 1`	Open management VLAN
`Sw2(config-if)#ip add 192.168.1.253 255.255.255.0`	Assigns IP Address of 192.168.1.253 to switch with a subnet mask of 255.255.255.0 in VLAN 1 for remote access
`Sw2(config-if)#no shut`	Enables the interface
`Sw2(config-if)#ip default-gateway 192.168.1.1`	Configure default gateway for the switch (Default Gateway is the IP Address of the Router)
`Sw2(config)#interface f0/1`	Moves to interface configuration mode
`Sw2(config-if)#switchport mode access`	Set f0/1 as Access link
`Sw2(config-if)#switchport access VLAN 5`	Assign f0/1 to VLAN 5
`Sw2(config-if)#no shut`	Enables the interface
`Sw2(config-if)#exit`	Returns to global configuration mode
`Sw2(config)#interface g0/1`	Moves to interface configuration mode
`Sw2(config-if)#switchport mode trunk`	Set g0/1 as a Trunk link
`Sw2(config-if)#switchport trunk allowed VLAN 1,5,10`	Allows VLAN 1,5 and 10 to travel across the trunk link
`Sw2(config-if)#switchport nonegotiate`	Prevents the specific interface in generating DTP frames
`Sw2(config-if)#no shut`	Enables the interface
`Sw2(config-if)#end`	Returns to privilege mode

At Router

Command	Description
`R1>en`	Moves to privilege mode
`R1#config t`	Moves to global configuration mode
`R1(config)#interface g0/0`	Moves to interface configuration mode
`R1(config-if)#Description Trunk Link to SW1`	(Optional) Sets locally significant description to the sub-interface
`R1(config-if)#no shut`	Enables the interface
`R1(config-if)#exit`	Returns to global configuration mode
`R1(config)#interface g0/0.1`	Creates sub-interface g0/0.1 and moves to sub-interface configuration mode
`R1(config-subif)#Description Default Gateway of Management VLAN 1`	(Optional) Sets locally significant description to the sub-interface

`R1(config-subif)#encapsulation dot1q 1`	Assigns VLAN 1 to this sub-interface. The sub-interface uses 802.1Q tagging protocol
`R1(config-subif)#ip add 192.168.1.1 255.255.255.0`	Configure default gateway for the sub-interface
`R1(config-subif)#exit`	Returns to global configuration mode
`R1(config)#interface g0/0.5`	Creates sub-interface g0/0.5 and moves to sub-interface configuration mode
`R1(config-subif)#Description Default Gateway of VLAN 5`	(Optional) Sets locally significant description to the sub-interface
`R1(config-subif)#encapsulation dot1q 5`	Assigns VLAN 5 to this sub-interface. The sub-interface uses 802.1Q tagging protocol
`R1(config-subif)#ip add 192.168.5.1 255.255.255.0`	Configure default gateway for the sub-interface
`R1(config-subif)#exit`	Returns to global configuration mode
`R1(config)#interface g0/0.10`	Creates sub-interface g0/0.10 and moves to sub-interface configuration mode
`R1(config-subif)#Description Default Gateway of VLAN 10`	(Optional) Sets locally significant description to the sub-interface
`R1(config-subif)#encapsulation dot1q 10`	Assigns VLAN 10 to this sub-interface. The sub-interface uses 802.1Q tagging protocol
`R1(config-subif)#ip add 192.168.10.1 255.255.255.0`	Configure default gateway for the sub-interface
`R1(config-subif)#exit`	Returns to global configuration mode

Inter-VLAN Routing on a Layer 3 Switch

Recall that the Router-on-a-stick provided the solution to the limitation that the legacy Inter-VLAN routing has. But, despite its effectiveness in the Inter-VLAN communication process, it still has a drawback, especially in the restriction of allowed VLANs. As such, the Router-on-a-Stick may be scalable but only to a limited number. In this section, we will discuss the more scalable and faster method in providing Inter-VLAN communication.

Inter-VLAN Routing through a layer 3 switch is the modern method for Inter-VLAN communication for it uses hardware-based switching to attain higher-packet processing rates than routers. This method uses the Switched Virtual Interface (SVI) that is configured on the Layer 3 switch.

The creation of an SVI is the same way as the configuration of creating a management VLAN interface. The SVI may be virtual, but its function for VLAN is the same as the capabilities of a router interface.

The following are some of the advantages brought by this method *(source: Cisco Networking Academy CCNA7 - SRWE Chapter 4 Module)*:

- Faster and more scalable than Router-on-a-Stick because everything is hardware switched and routed.
- There is no need for external links from the switch to the router for routing.
- Layer 2 EtherChannels can be used as trunk links between switches to increase bandwidth and is not limited to one link.
- Lower latency since data does not need to leave the switch to be routed to a different network.
- More commonly deployed in a Campus LAN compared to Routers.
- VLANs are routed using multiple SVIs.

Example:

Let us consider the figure on the right. The switch is connected to two computers on different Vlans. PC1 is in Vlan 5 and PC2 is in Vlan 10. Configure Inter-Vlan on layer 3 switch.

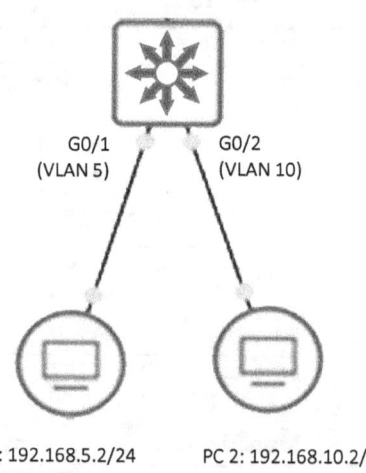

To achieve the right configuration for this type of network, the following steps are recommended for you to follow:

STEP 1: CREATE THE VLANS

`Sw1>`**`en`**	Moves to privilege mode
`Sw1#`**`config t`**	Moves to global configuration mode
`Sw1(config)#`**`VLAN 5`**	Creates VLAN 5
`Sw1(config)#`**`name LAN5`**	Set VLAN 5 name to LAN5
`Sw1(config)#`**`VLAN 10`**	Creates VLAN 10
`Sw1(config)#`**`name LAN10`**	Set VLAN 10 name to LAN10

STEP 2: CREATE THE SVI VLAN INTERFACES AND ASSIGN GATEWAY OF THE VLANS

Command	Description
`Sw1>en`	Moves to privilege mode
`Sw1#config t`	Moves to global configuration mode
`Sw1(config)#interface VLAN 5`	Creates a virtual interface for VLAN 5 and enters interface configuration mode
`Sw1(config-if)#ip add 192.168.5.1 255.255.255.0`	Assigns IP Address and Subnetmask
`Sw1(config-if)#no shut`	Enables the interface
`Sw1(config)#interface VLAN 10`	Creates a virtual interface for VLAN 10 and enters interface configuration mode
`Sw1(config-if)#ip add 192.168.10.1 255.255.255.0`	Assigns IP Address and Subnetmask
`Sw1(config-if)#no shut`	Enables the interface

STEP 3: CONFIGURE ACCESS PORTS AND VLAN MEMBERSHIP

Command	Description
`Sw1>en`	Moves to privilege mode
`Sw1#config t`	Moves to global configuration mode
`Sw1(config)#interface g0/1`	Moves to interface configuration mode
`Sw1(config-if)#switchport mode access`	Set interface to access mode
`Sw1(config-if)#switchport access VLAN 5`	Assign g0/1 to VLAN 5
`Sw1(config)#interface g0/2`	Moves to interface configuration mode
`Sw1(config-if)#switchport mode access`	Set interface to access mode
`Sw1(config-if)#switchport access VLAN 10`	Assign g0/2 to VLAN 10

STEP 4: ENABLE IP ROUTING

Command	Description
`Sw1>en`	Moves to privilege mode
`Sw1#config t`	Moves to global configuration mode
`Sw1(config)#ip routing`	Enables routing on the switch

If you intend that your VLANs be reachable to other layer 3 devices, VLANs must be advertised with the help of either static or dynamic routing.

The routing capability of layer 3 switches will not work unless a routed port is created. In order to configure a port to be a routed port, enter the following commands on the interface of the switch directly connected to the router.

`Sw1>`**`en`**	Moves to privilege mode
`Sw1#`**`config t`**	Moves to global configuration mode
`Sw1(config)#`**`interface g0/0`**	Moves to interface configuration mode
`Sw1(config-if)#`**`no switchport`**	Creates a layer 3 port on a switch

EtherChannel

CHAPTER 8

In the previous chapter, we Introduced that in actual network implementation, the best practice is to provide redundant links that will serve as a backup connection in case that one link fails. Considering the protocols under the loop avoidance, a network might have a redundant physical link. Still, its functionality is blocked due to the structure presented by the protocols such as the Spanning-Tree Protocol (STP) to avoid switching loops. Also, there are instances that the network requires more bandwidth than a single link can provide, and that need for a doubled link or more is needed to achieve a good performing and quality network.

This chapter will introduce the concept of link aggregation as a solution in providing a redundant working link.

EtherChannel Operation

A link aggregation protocol is a must for the STP not to block the redundant link existed on the network. In Cisco technology, this is referred to as EtherChannel.

EtherChannel is the technology that groups multiple physical links into a single logical link. In MikroTik, this is referred to as "Bonding". With EtherChannel, a network can attain fault-tolerance, load sharing, more bandwidth, especially increasing the overall speed of a switch-to-switch connection and redundancy between devices such as routers, switches, and servers.

The port created due to the EtherChannel configuration is called ***"port channel"*** which is a virtual interface caused by the bonding of two or more links. In case that a link fails within the domain of EtherChannel, traffic that was previously carried over by the failed link will transition to the remaining active links within the EtherChannel.

Figure 8-1. EtherChannel

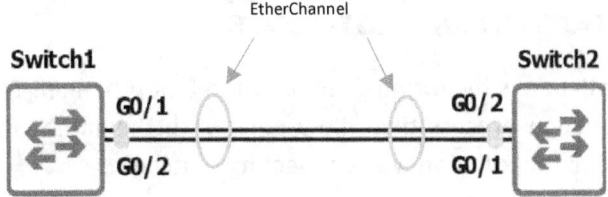

ADVANTAGES OF ETHERCHANNEL

(source: CCNA7 SRWE Chapter 6 Module, Cisco Networking Academy [netacad.com])

- Instead of entering the configuration task one by one on each port, the EtherChannel can be used instead to ensure consistency in the configuration throughout the links.
- Existing switch ports are the only thing the EtherChannel relies on. Therefore, there is no need to upgrade the link to a faster and more expensive connection to attain high bandwidth.
- There is load balancing between the links that are in the same EtherChannel.
- Link aggregation is created, making the physical interfaces be seen as one virtual link. If several EtherChannel groupings exist between two switches, STP blocks one group to avoid switching loops. When STP blocks one of the redundant links, it blocks the entire EtherChannel. With this, it blocks all the ports belonging to that particular EtherChannel link. And where there is only one EtherChannel link, all physical links in the EtherChannel are active since STP sees only one (logical) link.
- It provides link redundancy since the overall link is perceived as one logical connection. Moreover, the failure of one physical link within the channel does not alter the topology.

RESTRICTIONS IN THE IMPLEMENTATION OF ETHERCHANNEL

(source: CCNA7 SRWE Chapter 6 Module, Cisco Networking Academy [netacad.com])

- Only the same interface types can be mixed within an EtherChannel (Eq. GigabitEthernet with GigabitEthernet)
- Only Interfaces with the same media type can be mixed within an EtherChannel. (Eq. UTP cable with a UTP Cable)
- Currently, only eight (8) compatibly configured Ethernet ports can the EtherChannel support for bonding.
- Provides full-duplex bandwidth up to 800 Mbps (Fast EtherChannel) or 8 Gbps (Gigabit EtherChannel) between one switch and another switch or host.
- Cisco Catalyst 2960 Layer 2 switch currently supports up to six EtherChannels only.
- Consistency of port configuration on both sides must be observed when using EtherChannel.
- The Port Channel interface of the EtherChannel affects all the physical interfaces associated with it whenever configuration changes are made.

AUTO-NEGOTIATION PROTOCOLS

Negotiation is the forming factor of the EtherChannel. There are two protocols available for the negotiation process that allow ports with the same characteristics to form a channel through dynamic negotiation with connecting switches

- Port Aggregation Protocol (PAgP)
- Link Aggregation Control Protocol (LACP)

Port Aggregation Protocol

It is a Cisco proprietary protocol that aids the establishment of EtherChannel. What it does is that when the links used are in PAgP, packets are sent between EtherChannel capable ports to start the negotiation process in forming a channel. Once Ethernet links are matched determined by the PAgP, the links are bundled into an EtherChannel. When implemented in a switched network where Spanning-tree Protocol is running, is treated as a single port.

Packets under the PAgP are sent every 30 seconds. This is one way how the PAgP manages its link. Also, PAgP manages links for additions and failures in between two switches. Furthermore, it checks configuration consistency to ensure that all ports within the EtherChannel must have similar types of configuration such as having the same speed, duplex setting and VLAN information on both ends to assure compatibility, a key factor in enabling the link of EtherChannel. When changes are being made after the creation of its channel, the configuration is likewise on all ports in the channel is changed.

There are three (3) modes for PAgP, these are:

On	Even without Port Aggregation Protocol, this mode forces the interface into an EtherChannel but will not exchange PAgP packets. This is established only if both ends of the link are also in the **ON** mode.
PAgP desirable	The interface initiates negotiation with other interfaces by sending PAgP packets; as such, the interface is set into an active negotiating state.
PAgP auto	It sets the interface in a passive negotiating state, therefore it will only respond to PAgP packets, but there will be no negotiation to be initiated.

As a guide for the establishment of PAgP links, refer to the mode settings below.

Switch 1	Switch 2	Channel Establishment
On	On	Yes
On	Desirable/Auto	No
Desirable	Desirable	Yes
Desirable	Auto	Yes
Auto	Desirable	Yes
Auto	Auto	No

PAgP Configuration

Let us consider the below figure. Our task is to configure PAgP on both switches and verify its configuration.

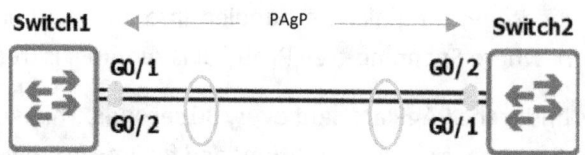

At Switch 1:

STEP 1. CONFIGURE PORT-CHANNEL

Sw1>**en**	Moves to privilege mode
Sw1#**config t**	Moves to global configuration mode
Sw1(config)#**interface range g0/1-2**	Moves to interface configuration mode selecting g0/1 and g0/2
Sw1(config-if-range)#**switchport mode trunk**	Set g0/1 and g0/2 as trunk link
Sw1(config-if-range)#**shutdown**	Disables the port g0/1 and g0/2
Sw1(config-if-range)#**channel-group 1 mode desirable**	Creates channel group 1 as PAgP channel and assigns interfaces g0/1 and g0/2 as ports of it.
Sw1(config-if-range)#**no shutdown**	Enables the PAgP channel
Sw1(config-if-range)#**exit**	Moves to global configuration mode
Sw1(config)#**interface port-channel 1**	Creates the port channel logical interface 1 and moves to interface configuration mode.
Sw1(config-if)#**switchport mode trunk**	Set port channel 1 as trunk link
Sw1(config-if)#**switchport trunk allowed VLAN 1,5,10**	Allows VLAN 1,5 and 10 to travel across the trunk link

To check that you have an active trunk link configured, issue the below commands:

```
Sw1# show interfaces trunk

Port      Mode      Encapsulation   Status      Native VLAN
G0/1      on        802.1q          trunking    1
G0/2      on        802.1q          trunking    1
```

> **Note:**
>
> *Interfaces to be added in the channel group must be shutdown first.*

At Switch 2:

`Sw2>`**`en`**	Moves to privilege mode
`Sw2#`**`config t`**	Moves to global configuration mode
`Sw2(config)#`**`interface range g0/1-2`**	Moves to interface configuration mode selecting g0/1 and g0/2
`Sw2(config-if-range)#`**`switchport mode trunk`**	Set g0/1 and g0/2 as trunk link
`Sw2(config-if-range)#`**`shutdown`**	Disables the port g0/1 and g0/2
`Sw2(config-if-range)#`**`channel-group 1 mode desirable`**	Creates channel-group 1 as PAgP channel and assigns interfaces g0/1 and g0/2 as ports of it.
`Sw2(config-if-range)#`**`no shutdown`**	Enables the PAgP channel
`Sw2(config-if-range)#`**`exit`**	Moves to global configuration mode
`Sw2(config)#`**`interface port-channel 1`**	Creates the port-channel logical interface 1 and moves to interface configuration mode.
`Sw2(config-if)#`**`switchport mode trunk`**	Set port-channel 1 as trunk link
`Sw2(config-if)#`**`switchport trunk allowed VLAN 1,5,10`**	Allows VLAN 1,5 and 10 to travel across the trunk link

To check that you have an active trunk link configured, issue the below commands:

```
Sw2# show interfaces trunk

Port      Mode      Encapsulation  Status       Native VLAN
G0/1      on        802.1q         trunking     1
G0/2      on        802.1q         trunking     1
```

STEP 2. VERIFY PORT CHANNEL 1 STATUS

```
Sw1# show etherchannel summary
Flags:  D - down         P - in port-channel
        I - stand-alone  s - suspended
        H - Hot-standby (LACP only)
        R - Layer3       S - Layer2
        U - in use       f - failed to allocate aggregator
        u - unsuitable for bundling
        w - waiting to be aggregated
        d - default port
```

```
Number of channel-groups in use: 1
Number of aggregators:           1

Group  Port-channel   Protocol    Ports
------+-------------+-----------+-----------------------------
--------
1      Po1(SU)        PAgP        G0/1(P)   G0/2(P)

Sw2# show etherchannel summary
Flags:  D - down         P - in port-channel
        I - stand-alone  s - suspended
        H - Hot-standby (LACP only)
        R - Layer3       S - Layer2
        U - in use       f - failed to allocate aggregator
        u - unsuitable for bundling
        w - waiting to be aggregated
        d - default port

Number of channel-groups in use: 1
Number of aggregators:           1

Group  Port-channel   Protocol    Ports
------+-------------+-----------+-----------------------------
--------
1      Po1(SU)        PAgP        G0/1(P)   G0/2(P)
```

> **Note:**
> *If ever the EtherChannel will not display after configuring the switches, shut down the interfaces on the EtherChannel and then enable it again.*

Link Aggregation Control Protocol

Another introduced bonding technology for communication medium is the IEEE 802.3ad, known as the Link Aggregation Control Protocol (LACP) that groups several ports into a single logical channel. With this protocol, switches are allowed to negotiate an automatic bundle by transmitting LACP packets to the other switches.

Its concept is similar to the PAgP of Cisco. Still, the advantage is that since it is an IEEE standard, this allows establishing communication in an EtherChannel manner with different networking vendors.

LACP has three (3) modes, these are:

On	Even without Link Aggregation Control Protocol, this mode forces the interface into an EtherChannel but will not exchange LACP packets. This is established only if both ends of the link are also in the **ON** mode.
PAgP desirable	The interface initiates negotiation with other interfaces by sending LACP packets; as such, the interface is set into an active negotiating state.
PAgP auto	It sets the interface in a passive negotiating state, therefore it will only respond to LACP packets, but there will be no negotiation to be initiated.

As a guide for the establishment of LACP links, refer to the mode settings below.

S1	S2	Channel Establishment
On	On	Yes
On	Active/Passive	No
Active	Active	Yes
Active	Passive	Yes
Passive	Active	Yes
Passive	Passive	No

LACP Configuration

Let us consider the below figure. Our task is to configure LACP on both switches and verify its configuration.

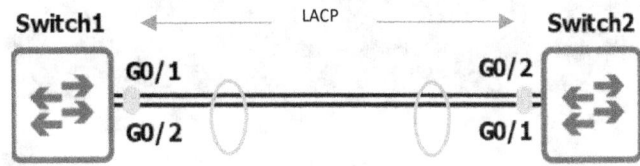

At Switch 1:

STEP 1. CONFIGURE PORT CHANNEL

`Sw1>`**`en`**	Moves to privilege mode
`Sw1#`**`config t`**	Moves to global configuration mode
`Sw1(config)#`**`interface range g0/1-2`**	Moves to interface configuration mode selecting g0/1 and g0/2
`Sw1(config-if-range)#`**`switchport mode trunk`**	Set g0/1 and g0/2 as trunk link
`Sw1(config-if-range)#`**`shutdown`**	Disables the port g0/1 and g0/2
`Sw1(config-if-range)#`**`channel-group 2 mode active`**	Creates channel group 2 as LACP channel and assigns interfaces g0/1 and g0/2 as ports of it.
`Sw1(config-if-range)#`**`no shutdown`**	Enables the LACP channel
`Sw1(config-if-range)#`**`exit`**	Moves to global configuration mode
`Sw1(config)#`**`interface port-channel 2`**	Creates the port channel logical interface 2 and moves to interface configuration mode.
`Sw1(config-if)#`**`switchport mode trunk`**	Set port channel 2 as trunk link
`Sw1(config-if)#`**`switchport trunk allowed VLAN 1,5,10`**	Allows VLAN 1,5 and 10 to travel across the trunk link

To check that you have an active trunk link configured, issue the below commands:

```
Sw1# show interfaces trunk

Port       Mode       Encapsulation   Status      Native VLAN
G0/1       on         802.1q          trunking    1
G0/2       on         802.1q          trunking    1
```

Note:

Interfaces to be added in the channel group must be shutdown first.

At Switch 2:

`Sw2>`**`en`**	Moves to privilege mode
`Sw2#`**`config t`**	Moves to global configuration mode
`Sw2(config)#`**`interface range g0/1-2`**	Moves to interface configuration mode selecting g0/1 and g0/2
`Sw2(config-if-range)#`**`switchport mode trunk`**	Set g0/1 and g0/2 as trunk link
`Sw2(config-if-range)#`**`shutdown`**	Disables the port g0/1 and g0/2
`Sw2(config-if-range)#`**`channel-group 2 mode active`**	Creates channel-group 2 as LACP channel and assigns interfaces g0/1 and g0/2 as ports of it.
`Sw2(config-if-range)#`**`no shutdown`**	Enables the LACP channel
`Sw2(config-if-range)#`**`exit`**	Moves to global configuration mode
`Sw2(config)#`**`interface port-channel 2`**	Creates the port-channel logical interface 2 and moves to interface configuration mode.
`Sw2(config-if)#`**`switchport mode trunk`**	Set port-channel 2 as trunk link
`Sw2(config-if)#`**`switchport trunk allowed VLAN 1,5,10`**	Allows VLAN 1,5 and 10 to travel across the trunk link

To check that you have an active trunk link configured, issue the below commands:

```
Sw2# show interfaces trunk

Port        Mode        Encapsulation  Status      Native VLAN
G0/1        on          802.1q         trunking    1
G0/2        on          802.1q         trunking    1
```

STEP 2. VERIFY PORT CHANNEL 2 STATUS

```
Sw1# show etherchannel summary
Flags:  D - down         P - in port-channel
        I - stand-alone  s - suspended
        H - Hot-standby (LACP only)
        R - Layer3       S - Layer2
        U - in use       f - failed to allocate aggregator
        u - unsuitable for bundling
        w - waiting to be aggregated
        d - default port

Number of channel-groups in use: 1
Number of aggregators:           1

Group  Port-channel  Protocol    Ports
------+-------------+-----------+-----------------------------------
------
```

```
2        Po2(SU)        LACP        Gig0/1(P) Gig0/2(P)


Sw2# show etherchannel summary
Flags:  D - down         P - in port-channel
        I - stand-alone  s - suspended
        H - Hot-standby (LACP only)
        R - Layer3       S - Layer2
        U - in use       f - failed to allocate aggregator
        u - unsuitable for bundling
        w - waiting to be aggregated
        d - default port


Number of channel-groups in use: 1
Number of aggregators:           1

Group  Port-channel  Protocol   Ports
------+-------------+----------+-----------------------------------
------

2        Po2(SU)        LACP        Gig0/1(P) Gig0/2(P)
```

In case that you want to use an LACP only for a group of interfaces (eq. G1/1 and G1/2) if the other switch is detected using LACP, use the **passive** LACP command.

Sw1>**en**	Moves to privilege mode
Sw1#**config t**	Moves to global configuration mode
Sw1(config)#**interface range g1/1-2**	Moves to interface configuration mode selecting g1/1 and g1/2
Sw1(config-if-range)#**switchport mode trunk**	Set g1/1 and g1/2 as trunk link
Sw1(config-if-range)#**shutdown**	Disables the port g1/1 and g1/2
Sw1(config-if-range)#**channel-group 3 mode passive**	Creates channel-group 3 as LACP channel and assigns interfaces g0/1 and g0/2 as ports of it.
Sw1(config-if-range)#**no shutdown**	Enables the LACP channel
Sw1(config-if-range)#**exit**	Moves to global configuration mode
Sw1(config)#**interface port-channel 3**	Creates the port-channel logical interface 3 and moves to interface configuration mode.
Sw1(config-if)#**switchport mode trunk**	Set port-channel 3 as trunk link
Sw1(config-if)#**switchport trunk allowed VLAN 1,5,10**	Allows VLAN 1,5 and 10 to travel across the trunk link

STEP 3. VERIFY PORT CHANNEL 2 AND 3 STATUS

```
Sw1# show etherchannel summary
<output omitted>
Number of channel-groups in use: 2
Number of aggregators:           2
Group  Port-channel  Protocol   Ports
------+-------------+----------+------------------------------------
2      Po2(SU)       LACP       Gig0/1(P) Gig0/2(P)
3      Po3(SU)       LACP       Gig1/1(P) Gig1/2(P)


Sw2# show etherchannel summary
<output omitted>
Number of channel-groups in use: 2
Number of aggregators:           2
Group  Port-channel  Protocol   Ports
------+-------------+----------+------------------------------------
2      Po2(SU)       LACP       Gig0/1(P) Gig0/2(P)
3      Po3(SU)       LACP       Gig1/1(P) Gig1/2(P)
```

Basic Telephony
CHAPTER 9

Introduction to Voice over IP

Voice over IP (VoIP) is responsible for transmitting voice communications and multimedia sessions over a network. It is a useful technology that helps the operation of businesses or organizations that is unique and has several features that are never found in a traditional telephone system. Each vendor has its exclusive features and capabilities. Some include integrated video call systems since some of the VoIP devices have their screen monitor embedded nowadays on the phone and have their structures ready for outgoing calls even outside the Local Area Network provided that an Internet connection is present.

VoIP runs over an IP network, which means it requires an IP address to be functional. Usually, for the VoIP phones to make calls, an IP PBX (Internet Protocol Private Branch Exchange) device is needed to connect the telephones to the public switched telephone network.

In the case of Cisco technology, some routers are capable of voice transmission over the network even without the presence of the IP PBX device. The only requirement is that you check if the firmware of your cisco router supports Voice. Make sure also to check the supported Cisco IP Phones of the firmware of the router. In this chapter, the configuration will only cover the basics of IP telephony and will be using Cisco 2800 series routers.

Voice VLAN

Unlike any other brand, Cisco has a special VLAN intended for Voice packets. The reason is that voice traffic requires a guaranteed bandwidth, a highly prioritized Quality of Service (QoS), the ability to avoid network traffic congestion, and a delay that should be less than 150ms from the source to the destination.

When network traffics are mixed, such as data and voice co-exist within a single path, there would be a tendency that the quality of voice transmission when making calls would be disrupted. As such, a barrier is created over a communication link. It is highly recommended for all network engineers and administrators always to consider special ports and links for voice.

In order to assign the port of the switch as Voice VLAN, the following commands are needed:

`Sw1>`**`en`**	Moves to privilege mode
`Sw1#`**`config t`**	Moves to global configuration mode
`Sw1(config)#`**`interface f0/1`**	Moves to interface configuration mode
`Sw1(config-if)#`**`switchport mode access`**	Set f0/1 as access link
`Sw1(config-if)#`**`switchport voice VLAN`** *`VLAN_id`*	Define the VLAN on which the voice packet will be handled

The voice VLAN features allow switch ports to transmit voice traffic with layer 3 preference and layer 2 classics of service (CoS) standards from an IP Phone. The switches are using cisco Discovery Protocol (CDP) to communicate with the IP Phone; for that reason, it is recommended to make sure that CDP is enabled on any switch port that is linked to an IP Phone.

> **Note:**
> *By default, Voice Vlans are disabled and that switch ports drops frames that are tagged in hardware.*

Voice and Data with Trust Configuration

The following commands are used for Cisco IP Phones that trust data traffic using the CoS originating from a computer connected to the IP Phone's access port. Native VLAN is what data traffic uses.

`Sw1>`**`en`**	Moves to privilege mode
`Sw1#`**`config t`**	Moves to global configuration mode
`Sw1(config)#`**`mls qos`**	QoS functionality is enabled globally
`Sw1(config)#`**`interface f0/1`**	Moves to interface configuration mode
`Sw1(config-if)#`**`mls qos trust cos`**	Interface's state is set to trust and will classify traffic by inspecting the CoS
`Sw1(config-if)#`**`mls qos trust dscp`**	Interface's state is set to trust and will classify traffic by inspecting the DSCP
`Sw1(config-if)#`**`switchport voice VLAN dot1p`**	The swill will be using IEEE 802.1p priority tagging to forward all voice traffic with a higher priority through the native VLAN

`Sw1(config-if)#switchport voice VLAN 10`	Define the VLAN on which the voice packet will be handled
`Sw1(config-if)#switchport priority extend trust`	Extends the state of trust to the computer connected to the VoIP Phone's access port.
`Sw1(config-if)#priority-queue out`	Voice packets are given head-of-line privileges when exiting the port to prevent jitter.
`Sw1(config-if)#spanning-tree portfast`	Enables PortFast that removes the interface from STP.
`Sw1(config-if)#spanning-tree bpduguard enable`	Enables BPDU guard on the Interface

Voice and Data without Trust Configuration

The following commands are used for Cisco IP Phones without trusting data traffic originating from a computer connected to the IP Phone's access port. The Data Traffic will use 802.1Q frame type.

`Sw1>en`	Moves to privilege mode
`Sw1#config t`	Moves to global configuration mode
`Sw1#config t`	QoS functionality is enabled globally
`Sw1(config)#interface f0/1`	Moves to interface configuration mode
`Sw1(config-if)#mls qos trust cos`	Interface's state is set to trust and will classify traffic by inspecting the CoS
`Sw1(config-if)#mls qos trust dscp`	Interface's state is set to trust and will classify traffic by inspecting the DSCP
`Sw1(config-if)#switchport voice VLAN 10`	Configures voice VLAN 10
`Sw1(config-if)#switchport access VLAN 20`	Configures data VLAN 20
`Sw1(config-if)#priority-queue out`	Voice packets are given head-of-line privileges when exiting the port to prevent jitter.
`Sw1(config-if)#spanning-tree portfast`	Enables PortFast that removes the interface from STP.
`Sw1(config-if)#spanning-tree bpduguard enable`	Enables BPDU guard on the Interface

Call Manager Express

The Call Manager Express (CME) is a technology integrated into the Cisco IOS as an enhanced IP telephony solution.

For the Cisco router to support your Cisco VoIP Phones, you must first load the IP Phone firmware onto the router. Use the following commands:

At Router:

```
R1>en
R1#config t
R1(config)#tftp server flash:[firmware filename]
```

Once the firmware is loaded, you need to reboot your router. Once powered on again, specify the Cisco IP Phone firmware file to use the Specific VoIP Phone when they register on the network. Use the following commands:

```
R1>en
R1#config t
R1(config)#load [phone-type][firmware type]
```

Next is to declare the IP address and the port number to be used by the CME in registering the IP Phones and providing their configuration:

```
R1>en
R1#config t
R1(config)#telephony-service
R1(config-telephony)#ip source-address [CME IP Address] port [port number]
```

> **Note:**
> By default, 2000 is the port for CME.

Lastly, you need to build the XML configuration files required and provide them to the IP Phones when they are registered. Use the following commands

```
R1>en
R1#config t
R1(config)#telephony-service
R1(config-telephony)#create cnf-files
```

Telephony Basic Configuration

Let us use the below topology as an example in order to setup telephony service in Cisco. Assume that the router is 2800 series model and that all of its firmware is loaded successfully. The IP Phone's model used in this example is 7960.

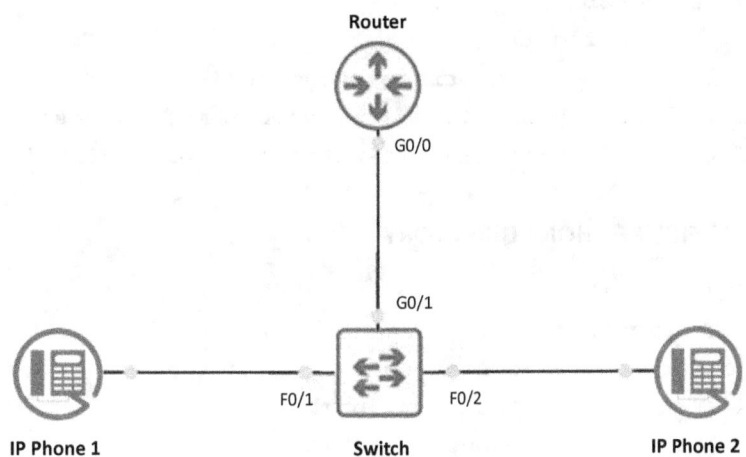

STEP 1: ASSIGN IP TO THE ROUTER

```
Router>enable
Router#config t
Router(config)#interface g0/0
Router(config-if)#ip address 192.168.1.1 255.255.255.0
Router(config-if)#no shutdown
```

STEP 2: CONFIGURE DHCP

```
Router>enable
Router#config t
Router(config)#ip dhcp pool voice
Router(dhcp-config)#network 192.168.1.0 255.255.255.0
Router(dhcp-config)#default-router 192.168.1.1
Router(dhcp-config)#option 150 ip 192.168.1.1
```

STEP 3: CONFIGURE CALL MANAGER EXPRESS (CME) TELEPHONY SERVICE

```
Router>enable
Router#config t
Router(config)#telephony-service
Router(config-telephony)#max-dn 5
```

```
Router(config-telephony)#max-ephones 5
Router(config-telephony)#ip source-address 192.168.1.1 port 2000
Router(config-telephony)#auto assign 4 to 6
Router(config-telephony)#auto assign 1 to 5
```

STEP 4: CONFIGURE VOICE VLAN AT SWITCH

```
Switch>enable
Switch#config t
Switch(config)#interface range f0/1-2
Switch(config-if-range)#switchport mode access
Switch(config-if-range)#switchport voice VLAN 1
```

STEP 5: CONFIGURE PHONE DIRECTORY

```
Router>enable
Router#config t
Router(config)#ephone-dn 1
Router(config-ephone-dn)#number 1001
Router(config-ephone-dn)#exit
Router(config)#ephone-dn 2
Router(config-ephone-dn)#number 1002
```

To test if it is running from IP Phone 1, initiate a call to IP Phone 2. With the configuration above, the IP Phone should ring.

To add more phones, you need to increase the number of maximum directories and maximum ephones on the router. Make sure to set the switch's ports to voice VLAN where the newly installed IP Phone is connected.

The best practice is to configure your network in a VLAN environment and set all the best parameters on switches when voice and data traffic are both present in the network.

Glossary

Access layer Is one of the three cisco hierarchical layer models where users are directly connected to the network.

Access link a link that is part of one VLAN and carries only untagged packets

Access method is a means of how devices or users access the network.

Acknowledgment is a verification message sent by a device to another device indicating that an event has occurred. It is abbreviated as ACK.

Address Learning is the process of learning the MAC address of a device connected in the network

Alternate Port backup port for the designated port when the other side is not a root port. It is in the Blocking state

Asymmetric Switching exists in a network environment when a client/server network traffic flows, wherein clients are communicating with the server simultaneously.

Backbone refers to the portion of the network that provides the primary path for traffic sent to and initiated from other networks.

BackboneFast provides fast convergence at the backbone level of the network when a change of Spanning-tree topology occurs.

Bandwidth Rated throughput capacity of a given network medium or protocol, the maximum amount of data that travels across a medium.

Binary a two-character numbering system that contains only ones and zeros.

Blocking a state in a bridged network. It won't forward frames, listens to BPDUs. All orts are in a blocking state by default when the switched is powered on

Bottleneck occurs when the path or link of a connection is smaller than needed

BPDU are hello packets sent out as multicast messages at definable intervals to exchange information among switches in the network.

Bridge is software-based which requires a configuration to fully interconnect the devices connected on its interface, while switches are hardware-based because it uses an ASICs chip to help make filtering decisions.

Bridge ID is 8 bytes long which includes the Priority and MAC address of the switch. All Cisco switches running IEEE 802.1D have a default priority of 32,768.

Broadcast a transmission methodology that propagates network frames to all connected nodes of the network

Broadcast domain is the area or group of devices that receive broadcast frames.

Broadcast storm is an undesirable event in which many broadcasts are sent concurrently across all network fragments. A broadcast storm uses substantial network bandwidth and, typically, causes network timeouts.

Buffer is a storage area of memory used to hold data while in transit temporarily.

CDP Cisco Discovery Protocol. A proprietary data link layer protocol developed by Cisco Systems. It shares information about other directly connected Cisco devices with their OS, version, and IP Address.

Cisco IOS Cisco Internet Operating System. The kernel and software of Cisco routers and switches.

CLI Command-Line Interface. A terminal line that allows you to configure devices.

Collision is the event that occurs when two nodes simultaneously transmit in Ethernet. When the message meets at the media, the frames from each node collide.

Collision domain is the area in which frames are propagated and have collided.

Collision window period where hosts check if the medium is free and no other is transmitting

Congestion occurs when the network carries more data than it can handle.

Convergence occurs when bridges and switches transition to either the forwarding or blocking state.

COS Classic of Service. Similar to Quality of Service (QoS) but in layer 2.

Cost is also known as path cost.

CRC Cyclic Redundancy Check. A methodology that detects errors, whereby the frame recipient makes a calculation by dividing the frame contents which a prime binary divisor and compares the remainder to a value stored in the frame by the sending code.

CSMA/CA Carrier Sense Multiple Access with Collision Avoidance. It is a multiple access method used by devices that senses the links to avoid collisions by beginning transmission only after the channel is sensed to be idle.

CSMA/CD Carrier Sense Multiple Access with Collision Detection. It is a multiple access method used by devices that senses the links to detect collisions by allowing the device to share cables but only sending frames one at a time.

Cut-through frame switching a switching technique that does not provide error checking.

Data Link Layer the second layer of the OSI model where switches and physical address can be found.

Designated Bridge is the bridge with the lowest path cost in a bridged network.

Designated Port selected on a per-segment (each link) basis, based on the cost to get back to root bridge for either side of the link. Designated ports are in the state of forwarding.

Designated Port selected on a per-segment (each link) basis, based on the cost to get back to root bridge for either side of the link. Designated ports are in the state of forwarding.

Destination Address is the recipient's address.

Distribution Layer one of the cisco hierarchical layer model. The middle layer guides you through designing, installing, and maintaining the hierarchical arrangement of Cisco networks.

DTP Dynamic Trunking Protocol. A Cisco proprietary protocol made for trunking negotiation as well as the type of encapsulation to be used between VLAN-aware switches

Dynamic VLAN in this method, a port is assigned to a particular VLAN ID automatically.

EtherChannel is the technology that groups multiple physical links into a single logical link.

Encapsulation is a technique used by layered protocols in adding header information in the Protocol Data Unit (PDU).

Encryption is transforming or converting data into a randomized alphanumeric character perceived as a scrambled form to prevent unauthorized access.

Ethernet is a media access method that allows all hosts to share the same bandwidth of a link.

FastEthernet is an Ethernet specification capable of handling a speed of 100Mbps.

Flat Network all segments belong to a single broadcast domain but have a separate collision domain since it is based per segment

Flooding happens when the destination is not listed on the table; thus, switches or bridges will transmit a copy of the frame to every interface except where the traffic originated.

Fragment Free Is a modified version of cut-through switching wherein it starts to forward a frame after the first 64 bytes (collision window) are received and checked when no collision occurred on it, since most of the time, a collision occurs within the first 64 bytes

Frame is the envelope in the network. When the destination is not listed on the table, thus switches or bridges will transmit a copy of the frame to every interface except on the interface where the traffic originated.

Full Duplex the capacity to send and receive information at the same time.

Half Duplex the capacity to send and receive information one at a time.

IP Address Internet Protocol Address. A 32-bit unique address that is grouped into 4 octets separated by dotted decimal. Every device in a network must have unique IP.

Layer 2 Switch a network switch that works in the second layer of the OSI layer model and can only do switching capabilities.

Layer 3 Switch is also known as a multi-layer switch. A network switch that combines the functionality of a router and a switch.

MAC Address Media Access Control Address. Refers to the physical or hardware address of a device.

Multiple Spanning-Tree Protocol Defined in IEEE 802.1s standard, is a protocol that allows multiple spanning-trees or instances for each VLAN onto a single physical network.

Non-designated Port a port in the Spanning-tree network that can't send frames.

NVRAM Non-volatile Random Access Memory that keeps the content unharmed while the device is powered off.

Packet is the layer 3 letters in a network that contains logical addresses.

QoS Quality of Service. Is a technology that manages data traffic in order to reduce packet loss latency and ensure network traffic performance.

Redundancy is the process of adding additional devices or links to assure that there is no single point of failure.

Rapid Spanning-Tree Protocol The Rapid Spanning-tree Protocol with an IEEE standard of 802.1W, was designed to address the network need for faster convergence of ports

Root Bridge is the switch or bridge in the network won by-election for having the lowest bridge ID.

Spanning-Tree Protocol STP is a layer 2 protocol that runs on Bridges and Switches. The specification of STP is IEEE 802.1D which is the standard used not just by cisco switches, also by other vendors.

Static VLAN This is the typical way of assigning ports to a VLAN but is the most secured. The administrator configures the assignment; because of this, it is easy for the administrator to monitor the user's movement within the network.

Switch a device that is responsible for distributing, filtering, flooding, and forwarding frames.

VLAN Virtual Local Area Network. Segregates and minimizes the broadcast domain by breaking it into smaller parts, meaning broadcast from other subnetwork should remain only within its vicinity and not affect other subnetworks.

VTP Virtual Local Area Network Trunking Protocol. Allows the administrator to make changes whether to add, delete, or rename VLAN names, which are then propagated to all switches.

Bibliography

Cisco Systems (2001). *Cisco Networking Academy Program: Second-Year Companion Guide.* Cisco Press.

Empson, S. (2016). *CCNA Routing and Switching Portable Command Guide.* Cisco Press.

Lamle, T. (2001). *Cisco Certified Network Associate Study Guide.* McGraw Hill.

Odom, W. (2019). *CCNA 201-301: Official Cert Guide Vol.1.* Cisco Press.

Paquet et al., 2001. Building Scalable Cisco Networks. Cisco Press.

Antoniou, S. (2008). *Cisco Call Manager Express IOS Feature for VoIP.* Retrieved from https://pluralsight.com

Certificationkits. (2017). *Cisco CCNA – PortFast & BPDU Guard.* Retrieved from https://www.certificationkits.com/cisco-certification/ccna-articles/cisco-ccna-switching/cisco-ccna-port-fast-a-bpdu-guard

Cisco Systems. (2020). *Catalyst 3560 Software Configuration Guide, Release 12.2(52)SE.* Retrieved from https://www.cisco.com/c/en/us/td/docs/switches/lan/catalyst3560/ software/ release/12-2_52_se/configuration/guide/3560scg/swmstp.html

Cisco Systems. (2019). *Understanding and Configuring Spanning Tree Protocol (STP) on Catalyst Switches.* Retrieved from https://www.cisco.com/c/en/us/support/docs/lan-switching/spanning-tree-protocol/5234-5.html

Cisco Systems. (2009). *Configure and Troubleshoot Cisco IOS Telephony Service (ITS).* Retrieved from https://www.cisco.com/c/en/us/support/docs/voice/h323/25100-config-troubleshoot-its.html

Cisco Systems. (2007). *Understanding Multiple Spanning Tree Protocol (802.1s).* Retrieved from https://www.cisco.com/c/en/us/support/docs/lan-switching/spanning-tree protocol/24248-147.html

Cisco Systems. (2007). *Spanning Tree Protocol.* Retrieved from https://www.cisco.com/c/en/us/tech/lan-switching/spanning-tree-protocol/index.html

Cisco Systems. (2007). *Configuring Spanning Tree PortFast, BPDU Guard, BPDU Filter, UplinkFast, BackboneFast, and Loop Guard.* Retrieved from https://www.cisco.com/c/en/us/td/docs/switches/lan/catalyst4000/82glx/configuration/guide/stp_enha.html

Learncisco. (2014). *Spanning-Tree Protocol Types.* Retrieved from https://www.learncisco.net/

courses/icnd-2/VLANs-and-spanning-tree/stp-protocol-types.html

Packet Tracer Network. (2020). *Packet Tracer 7.3 tutorial - IP telephony basic configuration*. Retrieved from https://www.packettracernetwork.com/tutorials/voipconfiguration.html

Shaik, S. (2015). CCNP Switch (300-115) Version 2.0: MSTP introduction

http://saturn.glyndwr.ac.uk/cisco/ccna/semester

https://sys.dias.ac.cy/www3/wp-content/uploads/cisco_rs_ite/ccna-r-s_ITN/course/module5

https://etutorials.org/networking

www.omnisecu.com

netacad.com

www.ingramcontent.com/pod-product-compliance
Lightning Source LLC
Chambersburg PA
CBHW081600220526
45468CB00010B/2706